VERSE FOR AGES

by

Bernie Morris

and

Colleen Thatcher
(Partners in Rhyme)

Published by Bronwyn Editions in the United Kingdom 2018
Copyright © Bernie Morris and Colleen Thatcher
http://www.bronwynbooks.co.uk

Cover Artist: © Linda Koperski
Photos courtesy of Bernie Morris and Colleen Thatcher
Cover background photo by Linda Koperski
Photos edited by Linda Koperski
Internal vignettes by Linda Koperski

Originally printed by
Lightning Source UK 2009

This edition March 2018

In loving memory of a very special lady:

Colleen Thatcher

Acknowledgements

With special thanks to Martin Newell of *The Sunday Express*, who has so kindly allowed us to include some of his excellent work.

Apart from each other, and those famous poets and anonymous ones included in this collection, we would especially like to thank all friends and family members who have contributed to the making of this book.
Namely: Barbara Euphan Todd; Cherie Saunders; Cheryl Lisa Flurry; Chris Thomson; Ciara Lloyd Delaney; Dave Brewster; Deborah Ehmann; Eammon Buckley; Elena Lucy Martin; Ellen Bennett; Jacqueline Patey; Jane Quittenton; Jill Shilvock; Justin Froud; Lawrence Palmer; Lilli Ellen Thomson; Madeleine Thomson, Margaret J. Robinson; Mary Lacey; Nina Laury; Pauline Phillips; Rosemary Glubb; Siobhan O'Conchubhair; Tony Bennett and Walter R. Brooks.

That your words may go on.

Contents
(by section)

Dedications

I hope you enjoy reading these poems as much as I enjoyed writing them. Going over them again has opened the floodgates and memories. I dedicate these poems to my mum and dad:
Elsie and Eddie Price.
They gave me so much encouragement as a child. Also to all the lovely people who inspired me to write them.

Colleen Thatcher

I would like to dedicate this book to the memory of
Colleen Thatcher
My long-term colleague, co-writer and friend.

Bernie Morris

INTRODUCTION

Poems, as we know, are quite hard to publicise
Unless you're a celebrity or have great big blue eyes!
Or if a well-known author you might have the luck to be
Then you'll find it easy, just like falling off a tree.

So, my good friend and I have decided what to do.
We know that people like to read and like to write them too.
Filthy-rich and famous is not how we want to be.
We only want to pass this on to friends and family.

We rooted through our files just to see what we had there.
The paperwork we found would have made a donkey swear.
We dusted off the cobwebs from the stuff we'd had for years
And found enough to keep you all in laughter, love and tears.

Next thing you know we typed it up-to-date
Edited and sorted and tweaked it into shape.
We said, at the printers is the place it ought'a be
They do it really quick these days, as you can surely see.

So for all our kids and friends and sibs and aunts and uncles too
Here's our legacy of verse, both old and some quite new.
There're happy, sad and pretty ones – a rhyme for every mood.
We've even thrown some funnies in, though none are very rude.

Enjoy...

Bernie and Colleen xx

Animals

For those innocents with whom we share the planet

A Cat Called Guinness

Guinness was a handsome cat
Named to suit her shades
Of beige and tan and chocolate brown
Dark as the Ace of Spades.

She'd often come to visit me
Five times a week or more
With charm and guile and subterfuge
She'd wait outside my door.

She'd purr her pretty head off
And if that didn't work
She'd start to mew most plaintively
She really was a berk!

But best of all was when I chose
These efforts to ignore
For then a large ungainly paw
Would pat against my door.

Melted by this cleverness
I'd always let her in
Like a furry cannonball
With a Cheshire Cattish grin.

A twirl or two around my legs
Would win her heart's desire
A bowl of milk, a slice of ham,
A warm place by the fire.

But then I'd have to shoo her out
Though she seemed inclined to stay
Her owner might have worried
If she stayed too long away.

Guinness was a lovely cat
Though fickle, worldly-wise
Her fur was darkest velvet
Eyes like mini apple-pies.

I often wonder where she went
For she don't come any more
I really miss her winsome wiles
And paw-pats on my door.

Bernie

Cheese Dream

There was a timid little mouse
Who lived beneath a flat.
A lump of cheese left out one night
Was guarded by the cat.
He gazed upon the lovely cheese
And sang this little ditty,
"Oh how I'd love to nibble that
If it weren't for that there kitty."

Bernie

The Dog

All day through, I guard this house
Nothing gets by me, not even a mouse.
The least little sound my ears detect
My hackles rise up to my neck.
I bark and warn all passers by
Come not near, come not nigh.
Don't dare touch the gate or door
You'll find yourself upon the floor.
Remember this is my domain
For my family I feel the same.
Don't come within these bounds
Or you'll answer to this hound.

Colleen

The Eagle

He clasps the crag with crooked hands;
Close to the sun in lonely lands,
Ring'd with the azure world, he stands.

The wrinkled sea beneath him crawls;
He watches from his mountain walls,
And like a thunderbolt he falls.

Alfred, Lord Tennyson

The Donkey

This was one of Colleen's favourites

When fishes flew and forests walked
And figs grew upon thorn,
Some moments when the moon was blood
Then surely I was born.

With monstrous head and sickening cry
And ears like errant wings,
The devil's walking parody
On all four-footed things.

The tattered outlaw of the earth,
Of ancient crooked will;
Starve, scourge, deride me: I am dumb,
I keep my secret still.

Fools! For I also had my hour;
One far fierce hour and sweet:
There was a shout about my ears,
And palms before my feet...

G.K. Chesterton

Five Eyes

In Hans' old mill his three black cats
Watch the bins for the thieving rats.
Whisker and claw, they crouch in the night,
Their five eyes smouldering green and bright:
Squeaks from the flour sacks, squeaks from where
The cold wind stirs on the empty stair,
Squeaking and scampering everywhere.
Then down they pounce, now in, now out,
At whisking tail, and sniffling snout;
While lean old Hans, he snores away
Till peep of light and break of day;
Then up he climbs to his creaking mill,
Out come his cats all grey with meal,
Jekkel, and Jessop and one-eyed Jill.

Walter De La Mare

The Fox and the Raven

A raven once perched in a tree.
In his beak was a portion of Brie,
Or maybe 'twas Roquefort;
He hadn't yet spoke, or
Reveal just what type it might be.

A fox sat below, and said smiling,
"Your feathers have beautiful styling;
"J'admire ton plumage."
(That was mere persiflage)
Such words are indeed, most beguiling.

It's unlikely that this will surprise
The reader observant and wise;
It's often been noted
A fox is devoted
To unblushingly flatter with lies.

"You'll forgive an obsequious clamour-tongue
But I'll bet you have often with glamour
sung.
I'm eager to hear
Your voice, loud and clear;
For a fan, would you trill
"Gotterdammerung'?"

That was all of the coaxing he needed,
And the crow, like a shot, then proceeded.
In flattery doused,
Sang the 'Jewel Song' from 'Faust',
Which was never done better than he did.

The reward of the fox's depravity
Was a sign of the Law of Earth's Gravity
As Newton showed well.
The cheese promptly fell,
To end up in the fox's gut cavity.

I'm embarrassed to add that the bird
Emphatic'ly uttered a word
Quite unfit for this forum,
But the fox, with decorum,
Replied only "Tut", so I've heard.

Although morals are oft paradoxes,
Which are better off kept in old boxes:
Where cheeses are served
After dinner's observed,
After dinner is too, what a fox is.

Donald Hall

The Goldfinch

Sweet little bird with a red satin face
Poised on a thistle with infinite grace.
Daffodil-yellow the flash on his wing
Feathers all perfect as jewels in a ring.

We watched from the window in breathless delight
For an exquisite moment and then he took flight.
I turned from the window, my spirits downcast
He came not again – 'twas too lovely to last.

"Look, Mummy, look!" cried my five-year-old son,
"A picture of Goldie – the very same one!
I've bought with my sixpence, dear Mummy and so
You can have your own goldfinch wherever you go!"

Thirty years have gone by since that long-ago day;
Many things have been lost or have vanished away
But the picture still hangs at the side of my bed.
The bird's gem-bright colours of yellow and red
Have faded a little, but I can yet see
My son's happy face as he gave it to me.

Rosemary Glubb

The Kingfisher

It was the rainbow gave thee birth,
And left thee all her lovely hues;
And as her mother's name was Tears,
So runs it in thy blood to choose
For haunts the lonely pools, and keep
In company with trees that weep.

Go you and, with such glorious hues,
Live with proud peacocks in green parks;
On lawns as smooth as shining glass,
Let every feather show its marks;
Get thee on boughs and clap thy wings
Before the windows of proud kings.

Nay, lovely Bird, thou art not vain;
Thou hast no proud, ambitious mind;
I also love a quiet place
That's green, away from all mankind;
A lonely pool, and let a tree
Sigh with her bosom over me.

William Henry Davies b.1871

Kitty

There was once an adventurous kitten
Who had never yet pounced, scratched or bitten.
When a spider did scuttle
At pace most unsubtle
The kitty was seriously smitten.

He gazed at this wonder with awe
As the spider its recklessness saw
Then stopped in its tracks
Like a work made of wax
While the kitten extended a paw...

Bernie

Marigold

She moved through the garden in glory, because
She had very long claws at the end of her paws.
Her back was arched; her tail was high,
A green fire glared in her vivid eye;
And all the Toms, though ever so bold,
Quailed at the martial Marigold.

Richard Garnett

Ode to a Spider

Arachne, dark Arachne,
How did you come to be
Princess of the Darkness
Webbed in mystery?

Lurking in the shadows
Within your silken lair
Until unwitting insect
Blunders in your snare.

To all the frantic tremors
You seem to pay no mind
Until at last the hunger burns
Like coiled spring you unwind.

With ticking feet and snapping jaws
You swoop to claim your prize.
Terrible Arachne,
I'm glad you're not *my* size.

Bernie

On the Death of a Favourite Cat
Drowned in a Tub of Gold Fishes

'Twas on a lofty vase's side
Where China's gayest art had dyed
The azure flowers that blow;
Demurest of the tabby kind,
The pensive Selima reclined,
Gazed on the lake below.

Her conscious tail her joy declared;
The fair round face, the snowy beard,
The velvet of her paws,
Her coat, that with the tortoise vies,
Her ears of jet, and emerald eyes,
She saw; and purred applause.

Still had she gazed; but midst the tide
Two angel forms were seen to glide,
The genii of the stream:
Their scaly armour's Tyrian hue
Through richest purple to the view
Betray'd a golden gleam.

The hapless nymph with wonder saw:
A whisker first, and then a claw,
With many an ardent wish,
She stretch'd in vain, to reach the prize
What female heart can gold despise?
What cat's averse to fish?

Presumptuous maid! With looks intent
Again she stretched, again she bent,
Nor knew the gulf between.
(Malignant Fate sat by, and smiled)
The slipp'ry verge her feet beguiled,
She tumbled headlong in.

Eight times emerging from the flood
She mew'd to every wat'ry God,
Some speedy aid to send.
No Dolphin came, no Nereid stirr'd:
Nor cruel Tom, nor Susan heard.
A fav'rite has no friend!

From hence, ye beauties, undeceived,
Know, one false step is ne'er retrieved,
And be with caution bold.
Not all that tempts your wand'ring eyes
And heedless hearts is lawful prize.
Nor all that glitters, gold..

Thomas Gray

Rocky the Dog

Sun pours into our garden
But no wagging tail is seen.
After fifteen years of friendship
There're only memories, where he's been.
Those shining eyes and old rough coat
Of us shouting when he barked
His soft old crumpled bed
You'd fall over in the dark.
I miss his pushing up against me
The big holes he used to dig.
I want to feel his snuffles
And his long fur against my leg
His pleading bark telling me
He wants his 'squeaky peg'.
No more will I hear him
There's a vacuum now he's gone
But in my heart he nestles
His nearness lingers on.

Colleen

Spiz

Spiz the parrot was a lovely bird
Always seen and seldom heard.
Someone somewhere gave him an unhappy past
But when his friends found him, he was happy at last.
Though he moved four times, he was always happy with them
There was light and music around his own little den.
He was joined by others in cages besides
Full of colour and noise, in their own little hides.
He saw faces and places, his joy new no bounds
Even when master and mistress weren't always around.
There was always someone to give him water and seed
A chat and some sweet corn was all that he'd need.
Living with them, happy and content
Always taken care of wherever he went.
Then he fell ill, no one knew why
He alone knew, he would soon say goodbye.
The lights kept fading, he tried hard to the end
To tell them he loved them; he was their friend.
Now he lies 'neath the Magnolia's shade
Leaving behind the memories he made.

Colleen (Gary's parrot)

The Tiger

Tiger, tiger, burning bright
In the forests of the night,
What immortal hand or eye
Could frame thy fearful symmetry?

In what distant deeps or skies
Burnt the fire of thine eyes?
On what wings dare he aspire?
What the hand dare seize the fire?

And what shoulder and what art
Could twist the sinews of thy heart?
And, when thy heart began to beat,
What dread hand and what dread feet?

What the hammer? What the chain?
In what furnace was thy brain?
What the anvil? What dread grasp
Dare its deadly terrors clasp?

When the stars threw down their spears,
And water'd heaven with their tears,
Did He smile His work to see?
Did he who made the lamb make thee?

Tiger, tiger, burning bright
In the forests of the night,
What immortal hand or eye
Dare frame thy fearful symmetry?

William Blake 1757-1827

The Unbrave Pilot

There was a young bear who would fly
In a real plane right up in the sky
His smart flying jacket
Had cost him a packet
He said "What a cool bear am I."
But sadly his plane came to grief
He escaped by the skin of his teeth.
He said, "As a test pilot
I'm one shrinking violet."
As he sat there and shook like a leaf.

Bernie

ASTRO

For all stargazers

Astro Types

Aries is the forward type
He doesn't lose his head
Except when charging headlong in
Where "Angels fear to tread".

Taurus has a pretty face
And likes her comfort best.
She'll eat you out of house and home
Then take the longest rest.

Gemini's the coolest guy
With the very latest view.
He quickly loses interest though
And moves to pastures new.

Cancer is the guardian type
A bit like Mother Hen.
She'll keep you safe beneath her wing
But you might not fly again.

Leo is the King of signs
He'll always run the show
But don't you steal his thunder
Simply bask within his glow.

Virgo is particular
She'll wear a worried frown
While she straightens up your tie
And dusts your shoulders down.

Libra's quite the charming type
With the world's most winning smile.
He'll get away with murder
With his easy-going style.

Scorpio's a *femme fatale*
Alluring, deep and haunting
But if you rouse her jealous streak
Her vengeance will be daunting.

Sagittarius is the restless one
With wanderlust galore
But if you stuff his head with books
He might remain on shore.

Capricorn's a cautious type
Who bides her time with care.
She'll reach the top eventually
With grey streaks in her hair.

Aquarius is different
From anyone you know.
With wilful independence
He will his own way go.

Pisces is a dreamer
Caring, sweet and kind
She'd really like to change the world
But can't make up her mind.

Bernie

Love of Aquarius

Aquarius calendar
How old am I?
I could be 92 next February
Though I won't admit to one day over 23.

Even after all the birthday cards
Are cut and shuffled
It's hard to figure why
I've aged at least 500 years
Since I stumbled into you.

Yet I still believe in fairy tales
Like the Princess and the Frog.
Perhaps I'm really only three or so?

You'll never guess how old I really am
But I'll tell you anyway
I was born the hour I met you
And when you left – I died
Today.

Jane Quittenton

The Masters

How beautiful the universe
What little we can see
The shimmering stars
The silver moon
The timeless melody.

Are we goldfish in a bowl
Doomed eternally
To swim around our little world
And think it is the sea?
And that we are the masters?

Bernie

Moon Goddess

When Selene walks the night
Hair pale as the cold moonlight
Eyes bright as the starlit sky
When Selene passes by
The whole world turns to silver.

Bernie

Secret Sock-Swiping Aliens

Somewhere deep in the galaxy
Away from calendars and clocks
There lives a strange race of beings
Who exist by eating odd socks.

Under the cover of darkness
Night after night they descend
To steal their way into baskets
And wayward socks apprehend.

I know it's true you don't see them
But nevertheless they exist.
If that's not the answer then tell me
Why so many socks become missed?

Mum shoves them into the washer
In sets of twin pairs every time
Then puts them all helter-skelter
In the drier or onto the line.

It's only when she is sorting
She suddenly finds some don't match,
Not rarely, sometimes ~ but *always*
She is missing some of the batch.

Those aliens must be chameleons
Altering their colours to fit,
To blend into the ironing
When you're after your clean PE kit.

Also their shape is amorphous
(Which means they have no set design)
Letting your visitors copy
All kinds of clothes off the line.

Do you know what I'm saying?
You might, any day, find yourself
Picking up, folding and placing
A strange alien on your linen shelf!

How can we stop these sock-eaters?
I've got one idea. Please don't scoff.
Here's the thought I've come up with:
No one must take their socks off!

Jill Shilvock

Virgo Rising

My Love in his attire doth show his wit;
It doth so well become him.
For all occasions he hath dressings fit
For Winter, Spring or Summer,
No detail doth he miss
With all his finery on.
But Beauty's self he is
With all adornment gone.

Adapted from "Madrigal" (1602)

BEAUTY

... is in the eye of the beholder

Bath

Bath, fair city of terraced stone
With curves and circles in symmetrical row.
This upsurge in my breast for you alone
To gaze in wonder and inwardly know.

From my childhood of long hot summers
In winters of fun, in snow and rain
To my youth full of pain and stirring murmurs
I shall never see and feel that way again.

The valley between those hills of green
The Romans saw when they found the spa
And sowed the seeds of glory seen
Brought their art to adorn from afar.

Through the ages came Nash, Allen and Wood
Each leaving their mark, richly bestowed.
Everything blending, elegantly good
From the warmth of the stone to where Avon flowed.

Now the abbey casts its shadow around
To all the passages, alleys and nooks
Across where a thriving commerce is found
Shops full of art, antiques, treasures and books.

Great Pulteney Street leads to its stylish end
To Sydney Gardens, full of shrubs and bridges
Where everyone meets everyone's friends
Down between the railway's tunnels and ridges.

To be beckoned by one so elegant
I fill with pride as I look around
Aching inside as miles apart I'm rent.
Oh, wondrous Bath to you I'm bound!

Colleen

Beauty

Turn a sudden corner and there you find
Beauty that is calming to the eye
But pain to the eye:
A feeling that takes your breath away
Then pain inside your soul will stay.

Colleen

Betsy Cottage

A cottage akin to warmth and love
Stands opposite the old Village School.
Echoes of children's long-forgotten cries
Faint sounds of rope and ball.

The cottage heart starts to beat again
Its new owners now lovingly restored.
Its eyes are agleam as it smiles to itself
And with a welcome throws open its doors.

It remembers the time childish laughter it heard
When the school was alive and full.
Maybe it will hear the same sounds again
This time within its own walls.

Colleen

Competition

Bending, stretching, hoeing, weeding
Colour, perfume, flowers seeding.
Summer bursts forth from spring
Creatures of the garden sing.
Then there in his hands the silver gleams
The treasured cup of all his dreams.

Englefield

Glory

The colours of the earth are told
Green and Blue and Brown and Gold.
The warmth of the sun, the buzz of the bees
The glorious flowers, the strength of the trees
Shiny rivers, swelling seas.
But what have we sent beneath those shining waves
Are we not digging our own graves?

Colleen

Meadow

There was once, where wild winds blow,
Beneath this thick relentless snow,
A field of green with meadow flowers
Where children sang and danced for hours.
Who would think battling this dense cold,
Making this time, so very old,
The air was full of song and sun,
And tiny paths, where rabbits run.
Humming of pollen-covered bees,
A joyful time for all to see,
Never thinking that so very soon,
All would be still and cold beneath winter's moon.

Colleen

Memories

The river flows; the sun shines down
Midges dancing all around.
Ducks a-dabbling, reeds a-quiver
Oh! The peace of tranquil river.
Hands locked loosely swinging low
Faces smiling, eyes aglow.
Hearts go soaring, thoughts are fleeting
Never will we forget this lovers' meeting.
Lips brushed softly, light breath sighing
The distant sound of moorhens crying.
Soon we'll wend our separate ways
But memories live on of youthful days.

Colleen

My County

Berkshire on a spring day
A breeze lifting the leaves of May.
Soft green grass, down by the river
Seeing dragonflies a quiver.

Berkshire on a summer's morn
Bleating sheep, newly shorn.
Haystacks in the blazing sun
Going home after day's work done.

Berkshire in the autumn time
All flowers and fruits made into wine.
Hedgerows now made of golden trees
Glowing reds of shimmering leaves.

Berkshire on a winter's night
Snow outside, shining bright.
Stretching away across the Downs
Still and quiet, not a sound.

Berkshire here within my heart
Where every season plays a part.
Beauteous brick in street and lane
Shines the county of Royal fame.

Colleen

Seeing
I found a wondrous feeling
Looking at the scene.
A feeling of belonging
Of always having been.
Cygnets on the river
Butterflies in fields.
A mass of golden daffodils
Amid the vales and hills.

Colleen

Our Garden
The garden gate swings open
Showing Snowdrops under hedge
Clumps of golden Narcissi
A Robin hops upon a ledge.
Softly silver catkins hang.
Then God's gift
Of coming springtime
Comes across the land.

Summer sun warms crazy paving paths
Garden colours, brightly glowing.
Dragonflies on water darting
Full blown blossoms showing.
The heartbeat of our garden
Becomes a living thing
As perfumes, bees and spider webs
Bring long warm evenings to an end.

Now a myriad berries in clusters hang
Sun-thirsty grass quickly gulps the falling rain.
Then crisp fallen leaves and shiny apples glisten
As the sun comes out again.
Early morning webs cling round eager faces
As we inhale damp earthy odours

Collecting baskets full of harvest
Lifting high on suntanned shoulders.

All winter through
The evergreen sentinels
Resist the icy blasts
The glossy leaves and ferny bough
Memories of summer still last.
There's silence in our garden now.

Colleen

Remembered Garden

Here in this deep remembered garden,
I feel a dream full of pain.
I hear birdsong in the woods at evening
My youth is here with me again.

Colleen

Ruin

There was once a house where that old ruin stands
A fine bright building gazing over its lands.
Now ivy grows over its paneless eyes
With no blue reflected from the skies.
The doors on rusty hinges hang
In heavy winds, you hear them bang.
No more footsteps clatter these halls
No colour now on shapeless walls.
Tall chimneys crumbled into dust
Pump and cistern thick with rust.
It needs some heaven-sent soul
Who will now fight to make it whole.
Where is that one so filled with pride?
Who'll save this old house that almost died?

Colleen Price

Seaside

Sand and sea, sun and air
Seagulls crying everywhere.
Distant shouts and squeals of glee
Children bobbing in the sea.
Laughing faces, tanned and glowing
Lots of shiny bodies showing.
Warm brown limbs, eyes that shine,
This will linger on – always mine.

Colleen

Sometime

Up in the sky is a stormy cloud
A cloud with a threatening look.
Huge and thick, like a layer of smoke
Black like a layer of soot
Spread like an umbrella over the roofs.
Underneath, the gardens grow grey
Chilling the flesh as the deep shadows fall
Taking the light from the day.
Unmoving at first sight
Like trouble that darkens life
And changes life overnight.
But a lovely cloud though it's dark and cold
There's glory behind it now; I can see edges of gold.

Colleen Price

Sonnet

Shall I compare thee to a Summer's day?
Thou art more lovely and more temperate:
Rough winds do shake the darling buds of May,
And Summer's lease hath all too short a date:
Sometime too hot the eye of heaven shines,
And often is his gold complexion dimm'd;
And every fair from fair sometime declines,
By chance or nature's changing course untrimm'd:
But thy eternal Summer shall not fade
Nor lose possession of that fair thou owest;
Nor shall Death brag thou wanderest in his shade,
When in eternal lines to time thou growest:
So long as men can breathe, or eyes can see,
So long lives this, and this gives life to thee.

William Shakespeare

Upon Westminster Bridge

Earth has not anything to show more fair;
Dull would he be of soul who could pass by
A sight so touching in its majesty:
This City now doth like a garment wear
The beauty of the morning; silent, bare,
Ships, towers, domes, theatres, and temples lie
Open unto the fields, and to the sky;
All bright and glistening in the smokeless air.
Never did sun more beautifully steep
In his first splendour valley, rock or hill;
Ne'er saw I, never felt, a calm so deep!
The river glideth at his own sweet will:
Dear God! the very houses seem asleep;
And all that mighty heart is lying still!

William Wordsworth

(We wonder if he'd still be of the same opinion these days.)

CHILDREN'S

The following poems have been written either by children
or for them

After All

Oh NO – Mum, the drawer!
It's on the floor.
Don't shout Mum
'Cos I'm only four.
Mum, Mum – the flowers
They're on the floor!
Don't shout Mum
After all I'm only four.
Mum, Mum! Uh OH...

Cheryl Lisa Flurry

Beetle

If you find a beetle-bug
Struggling on its back,
Don't be mean and squash it;
It's having an attack.
Take a stick and gently
VERY gently mind
Flick the beetle over
Then its feet will find.

Bernie

Cat and Mouse

The cat of the house
Saw a very big mouse.
He ran a race to the book-case
And out he took a very big book.
On the front of the book
He took
It said, "How to catch a mouse
in a very big house.
All you have to do is hide in the loo
And when he comes past
Run out very fast
Stamp on his head until he goes red
Then have roast mouse
Next day in the house."

Lawrence Palmer (8)

Christmas Wish

I wish it was Christmas all through the year
So many people full of good cheer
Bright smiling faces wherever you go
The words "Merry Christmas!" ring to and fro.
Shops full of glitter and bright sparkling trees
Crammed full of goodies, aiming to please
Snow if we're lucky to set the scene
Just like a Christmas card, magic, serene.
Gifts in your stocking and more by the tree
Turkey for dinner, jelly for tea.
Aunties and uncles and neighbours pop in.
Dad's on the beer and Mum's sipping gin.
Nobody minds if you eat all the chocs
The grown-ups are busy – all watching the box.
And when like all good things it comes to an end
I wish it was Christmas all over again.

Bernie Bennett

Dragon

It lies in its cave
Sleeping on gold
The eternal old dragon
Fearless and bold.

No other can match
Its size or its strength
Its gleaming red eyes
Or fabulous length.

It dreams of the past
Of maidens and knights
Of castles and horses
Of swords and of fights.

It dreams and remembers
Its numerous fights
No sword and no shield
Just its fire gleaming bright.

Sleep, Old Dragon
And dream of the past.
No more battles or wars
Have peace at last.

Justin Froud (age 12)

Humpty

Humpty Dumpty sat on the fence
He really should have had more sense.
All the king's horses and all the king's men
Couldn't assemble his two halves again.

Humpty Dumpty sat on a rock
Then Humpty Dumpty got quite a shock.
There came a giant chicken upon a giant horse
She thought him a beauty
And hatched him – of course!

Bernie

Interruptions

"I wish," said Susan, "when I play pretending,
When I'm a knight, a hero, or a queen,
They wouldn't say, 'Your overall needs mending!'
They wouldn't say, 'Your hands are never clean!'"

"I wish, I wish," said Susan, "when I'm sitting
Proudly as Helen by the shores of Greece
They wouldn't say, 'Oh Susan, fetch my knitting –
I left it on the nursery mantelpiece!'"

"I wish," said Susan, "when I find a casket
Brimming with gold and jewels of the crown
They wouldn't say, 'That's Granny's mending-basket.
I told you not to touch it. Put it down!'"

"I wish," said Susan, "when the shadows flicker
And I and all my merry men have supped
And in the shrubbery the trees seem ever thicker,
I wish, I wish they wouldn't interrupt!"

Barbara Euphan Todd

Jack and John

Jack Spratt was much too fat
John Spratt was far too lean
And so between the two of them
They made a dreadful scene.
Jack Spratt got stuck inside the door
While John fell down a drain
And what with all the noise they made
The neighbours did complain.

Bernie

Ladies

Ladies dancing,
Stretching up and prancing
They are always glancing
Powdering their noses
Looking at their toeses.
Listen to them talking
Whenever they are walking.
Ladies, ladies all day long.

Cheryl Lisa Flurry

Matilda, (Who told Lies, and was Burned to Death).

Matilda told such dreadful lies,
It made one gasp and stretch one's eyes;
Her aunt, who, from her earliest youth,
Had kept a strict regard for truth,
Attempted to believe Matilda:
The effort very nearly killed her,
And would have done so, had not she
Discovered this infirmity.
For once, towards the close of day,
Matilda, growing tired of play
And finding she was left alone,
Went tiptoe to the telephone
And summoned the immediate aid
Of London's noble Fire-Brigade.
Within an hour the gallant band
Were pouring in on every hand,
From Putney, Hackney Downs and Bow,
With courage high and hearts a-glow
They galloped, roaring though the town,
"Matilda's house is burning down"
Inspired by British cheers and loud
Proceeding from the frenzied crowd,
They ran their ladders through a score
Of windows on the ball-room floor;
And took peculiar pains to souse
The pictures up and down the house,
Until Matilda's aunt succeeded
In showing them they were not needed
And even then she had to pay
To get the men to go away!
It happened that a few weeks later
Here aunt was off to the Theatre
To see that interesting play
The Second Mrs Tanqueray.
She had refused to take her niece

To hear this entertaining piece:
A deprivation just and wise
To punish her for telling lies.
That night a fire did break out–
You should have heard Matilda shout!
You should have heard her scream and bawl,
And throw the window up and call
To people passing in the street–
(The rapidly increasing heat
Encouraging her to obtain
Their confidence)–but all in vain!
For every time she shouted "Fire!"
They only answered "Little Liar!"
And therefore when her aunt returned,
Matilda, and the house, were burned.

By Hilaire Belloc

Miss Know-it-All

I knew a girl
She had lots of pearls.
They all called her
Miss Know-it-All.
She hated it
And she hated THEM.

Nina Laury

Old Mother Hubbard

She went to the cupboard
To fetch her poor dog some meat
But sadly for Rex
She'd forgotten her specs
So the poor dog got served pickled beet.

Bernie

The Queen of Suns

She made some buns
All on an Easter Day
The Knave of Suns
Stuck to his guns
And stole those buns away.
The King, irate, said
"Just you wait!
I'll give that boy the sack!"
The Knave was grave, and sick of buns
He brought the cold ones back.

Bernie

Queen's Song

Nobody ever tells me;
Nobody lets me know.
Wars are fought and groceries bought
And people come and go.
But what is the use of being a Queen
To sit in a marble hall
If nobody tells you anything,
Any-thing at all?

I want to know all the gossip
That all the courtiers know,
Who had a fight and stayed out all night
And who has a brand new beau.
But you sit on a throne and you're all alone
And if anyone comes to call
They simply won't tell you anything,
Anything at all.

Walter R. Brooks

Rum
I like rum.
It warms my tum
When I run.
I just *love* rum
When I feel numb
Whenever guests come
I just love rum.
Cheryl Lisa Flurry

Old Lady

I can see an old lady over there
She sits on the bench with long straggly hair.
She looks through her glasses, staring at you
Her name to the town is "Old Lady Sue".
She sleeps in the park, under the slide
Not really knowing where she can hide.
Her cheeks are so pale they are almost white
She strolls through the town by day and by night.
She takes all abuse – they call her a hag
And she carries her wealth in two carrier bags.
Cheryl Lisa Flurry

Shooting Star
Shooting star, burning bright
In the middle of the night
Zooming through the galaxy
On your way to me, to me.
I'll wish a wish before you die
And tumble down the starry sky
That once again one magic night
I might see you burning bright.
Cheryl Lisa Flurry

Silly Snow

(Lilli was asked to write a poem about snowflakes; she can sing it too)

Slowly falling
Winter's dawning
Autumn comes to rest.
Grab a hot –
Big cup o' cocoa,
Must put on my vest.
A nice cup o' tea
Is waiting for me
Home at old Loch Ness.
Too much on my Christmas list
Causing me lots of stress.
Tiny snowflakes,
Landing on lakes,
Getting in my hair.
One more throw
Before I go
To the snowflake fair.

Lilli Ellen Thomson, aged 10

Sixty Royal Pence

Sing a song of sixty pence
For a packet soup
Four and twenty chickens
Escaped from the coop
When the coop was opened
The queen began to cry
"What *can* we have for dinner now?
We can't have chicken pie!"
They went out to a restaurant
The king had fish and chips
The queen had champagne cocktail
Sipping dainty sips.
The maid was in the garden
Mowing up the lawn
When four and twenty chickens
Strode in and yelled for corn.

Bernie

Solomon Grundy

Born on a Monday,
Christened on Tuesday,
Married on Wednesday,
Took ill on Thursday,
Worse on Friday,
Died on Saturday,
Buried on Sunday.
This was the end
Of Solomon Grundy.

Stargazer

The stone age child who cannot sleep
He gazes at the stars
So high and bright above the night
He wonders what they are.
He thinks they might be spirits
Flying in the sky.
He thinks they might be watching him
A thousand peeping eyes.
He crawls back to his fire-lit cave
And snuggles in his fur
So glad he's firmly on the ground
Not all alone up there.

Bernie

The Sun

The sun shines upon us all
As it gets light the shadows fall.
Whilst in the sun the flowers grow
I've seen them grow, I'm sure, I know.
The sun we use for light and heat
But sometimes it's just too bright.
It reflects off silver, mirrors and brass
Glowing most when it reflects off glass.
Even though it's all so nice
Next time it's shining, just think twice.
We don't know what's going on out there
Next time it's shining, please, please don't stare.

Elena Lucy Martin

The Tooth Fairy

When a baby tooth falls out
Don't throw it away
Show it to your Mother
This is what she'll say
"Let's wrap it up in silver
Kitchen foil will do
Now underneath your pillow
Not too close to you.
Tooth Fairy will come tonight
Only while you sleep
She cannot come at all, you see
If you try to peep.
Fairies need your baby teeth
So pretty, small and white
To build their magic castles
All shining pearly bright.
So go to sleep my little one
And shut your eyes so tight
The Fairy sees the silver
Gleaming in the night
And in the morning you will see
She has paid you honestly
A silver coin so bright."

Bernie

Welly Boots

Dad has great big welly boots
For squishing in the mud;
Two great big black welly boots:
Thud, thud, thud.

Mum has got big welly boots,
Though not as big as Dad's;
Two big green welly boots
For when the weather's bad.

Big brother has big welly boots,
Though not as big as Mum's;
Two big blue welly boots
For when the raining comes.

I've got big welly boots,
Though not as big as bruv's;
Two big red welly boots,
For jumping in puddles I loves.

Siobhan O'Conchubhair

Wynken, Blynken, and Nod

Wynken, Blynken, and Nod one night
Sailed off in a wooden shoe –
Sailed on a river of crystal light
Into a sea of dew.

"Where are you going, and what do you wish?"
The old man asked the three.
"We have come to fish for the herring-fish
That live in this beautiful sea;
Nets of silver and gold have we,"
Said Wynken, Blynken, and Nod.

The old moon laughed and sang a song,
As they rocked in the wooden shoe;
And the wind that sped them all night long
Ruffled the waves of dew:

The little stars were the herring-fish
That lived in the beautiful sea.
"Now cast your nets wherever you wish –
Never afraid are we!"
So cried the stars to the fisherman three,
Wynken, Blynken, and Nod.

All night long their nets they threw
To the stars in the twinkling foam –
Then down from the skies came the wooden shoe,
Bringing the fishermen home:

'Twas all so pretty a sail it seemed
As if it could not be;
And some folk thought 'twas a dream they'd dreamed
Of sailing that beautiful sea;
But I shall name you the fishermen three:
Wynken, Blynken, and Nod.

Wynken and Blynken are two little eyes,
And Nod is a little head,
And the wooden shoe that sailed the skies
Is the wee one's trundle-bed.

So shut your eyes while Mother sings
Of wonderful sights that be,
And you shall see the beautiful things
As you rock in the misty sea
Where the old shoe rocked the fishermen three:-
Wynken, Blynken, and Nod.

CHRISTMAS

Both funny and festive

Christmassy Things

Starlight comes early on rooftops all snowy
Shops full of tinsel with windows all glowy
Letters to Santa and carols to sing
These are a few lovely Christmassy things.

Mangers and reindeer and sleighbells that tinkle
Christmas trees shining with baubles that twinkle
Fairies in chiffon with white sparkly wings
These are *more* favourite Christmassy things.

Garlands and lanterns in rooms decked with holly
Big stores that all have one Santa so jolly
Christmas night sleepless to see what he brings
These are some more of my Christmassy things.

Christmas Day dawning with hundreds of goodies
Presents and turkey and cream with your puddies
Mum and Dad smiling, while near church bell rings
These are my favourite Christmassy things.

When the frost bites, when the wind blows
When I'm feeling sad
I simply remember these Christmassy things
And then I don't feel so bad.

Bernie

Infant Nativity

The day of the Nativity
At school, at last was here
And teachers dressed the tiny tots
In clothes they had to wear.

Most infants wore a long white robe
With pretty tinsel haloes
And each one had a fluffy toy
To carry to the stable.

There was Joseph, Mary, angels
With silver foil-wrapped wings;
Shepherds and kings with gold card crowns
Who carried offerings.

One of the angel's halo slipped
And one had bent his wing.
Another wanted toilet when
It came the time to sing.

A small king dropped his bag of gold –
Shepherds waved and chattered.
The angel choir sang out of tune
But nothing really mattered.

Mums and dads all watched with pride –
A smile, a tear, a laugh
And at the end a vote of thanks
And flowers for the staff.

Pauline Phillips

Lament of the Christmas Tree Fairy

I am the Christmas Tree Fairy
Yes, I am the Star of the Show
On top of the Tree
For all to see
I'm Queen of the Castle, you know.

My dress is all sparkle and glitter
My hair is a cloud of white fluff
Every bauble reflects me
Lights winking offset me
You'd really think that was enough.

My working conditions are easy
Just one month in twelve every year
I'm loved and adored
That is my reward
No-one notices glittery tears.

The rest of the year I'm stuck in a box
Alone in the dark, spooky loft
A genuine Fairy
Would find this quite scary
With a wave of her wand – she'd be off!

What reason have I got to grumble?
And why my expression so glum?
Well, so might yours be
If you were like me
With a Christmas tree stuck up yer bum!

Bernie

The Night before Christmas

'Twas the night before Christmas and Santa's a wreck,
How to live in a world that's politically correct?
His workers no longer would answer to "Elves"
It seems "Vertically Challenged" they were calling themselves.

And labour conditions up at the North Pole
Were said by the Union to stifle the soul.
Four reindeer had vanished with much propriety,
Released to the wilds by the Humane Society,

And the EEOC had just made it quite clear,
That Santa had better not use JUST reindeer.
So Dancer and Donner and Comet and Cupid
Were replaced with four pigs, and you know that looked stupid.

The runners had both been removed from his sleigh,
The ruts were too dangerous, intoned EPA.
And people had started to call for the cops
When they heard prancing noises on their own rooftops.

Even smoke from his pipe had the people quite frightened
And his fur-trimmed red suit was called "Unenlightened"
And to show you the strangeness of life's ebbs and flows
Rudolph sued the old man for the use of his nose.

He had gone on TV and in front of the nation
He had cried out to Oprah for due compensation.
So half of the reindeer were gone and his wife
Who suddenly said she was sick of this life,

Joined a self-helping group and then left in a whiz
Demanding from now on her title was Ms.
And as for the gifts he had nary a notion,
That making a choice could cause such a commotion.

Nothing of leather and nothing of fur
Which meant nothing for 'him' and nothing for 'her'.
Nothing that might be construed to pollute
Nothing to aim at and nothing to shoot.

Nothing that clamoured or made lots of noise,
Nothing for JUST girls or JUST for the boys,
Nothing that claimed to be gender specific.
Nothing too warlike or too non-pacific.

No candy or sweets; they are bad for the tooth.
Nothing that seemed to embellish a truth.
And fairy tales, too, while they're not yet forbidden
Were like Barbie and Ken...they were better off hidden.

No baseball no football; someone could get hurt.
Besides, playing sports exposed kids to the dirt.
Dolls were too sexist and should be passé,
Nintendo 'twas found, rots your brain cells away.

So Santa just stood there, dishevelled, perplexed.
He just couldn't figure out what to do next.
He tried to be merry, he tried to be gay,
But you've got to be careful with that word, they say.

His sack was quite empty, laying limp on the ground;
No suitable gift for this year could be found.
Something special was needed, a gift that he might
Give to all without angering the left or the right.

A gift that would satisfy with no indecision,
Each group of all people in every religion
Every ethnicity, each colour and hue
Everyone, everywhere, yes, even you.

So he spoke his one gift with a price beyond worth...
"May you and your loved ones enjoy peace on this earth."

Internet

More Nights Before

'Twas the night before Christmas all over the flat
Not a creature was stirring except for a gnat.
It bit all the children
The Dad and the Mum
Then bit Father Christmas
Right on the bum!

'Twas the night before Christmas all over the flat
Not a creature was stirring 'cept one naughty cat.
He nicked all the turkey
And cream devoured quick
Then saw Father Christmas
Who gave him a kick.

'Twas the night before Christmas all over Penryn
Not a creature was stirring except for Bronwyn
She crunched all the holly
And munched mistletoe
Then said, "Oh baa golly!
I feel so weird-O."

'Twas the night before Christmas in Festiniogg
Not a creature was stirring except for one dog.
He chewed all the presents
And poo'd on the rug
Then slept by the children
Expecting a hug.

Bernie

DREAMS

Dreams come true if you want them to
If you want them to then it's up to you
Grow, grow the lightning tree
Never give in too easily

Francis Stevens

The Dream

Red lightning sparking leaden skies
Flickering fast – too fast for eyes.
Grey mud stretches far as I can see
No sign of the sea – where *is* the sea?

Gulls looking upward, beaks open wide
Fear in small black eyes; no place to hide.
Soaring and wheeling they scream their fright
One creases my hair in erratic flight.

Big as a swan it seemed when near
I stand and watch but feel no fear.
But now returns the forgotten sea
Smooth as black glass, it comes for me.

I turn to climb back up the shore
The sloping shingle is no more.
Instead I find a sheer cliff face.
How did I come to this mad place?

I try to scale this awesome wall
My limbs are numb – I *know* I'll fall.
I hear the roaring in my head
The sea is here, I'll soon be dead!

I have no voice yet try to scream
I wake and think "that same old dream...
What does it mean?"

Bernie

Dream Baby

Last night I dreamed again about the Baby—
The baby who is mine in all my dreams.
I don't know who he is or what his name is
But in my arms so natural he seems.

Is he the little one I lost so many years ago?
Is he trapped within my soul – nevermore to grow?
His eyes are blue
His smile is sweet
He never seems to cry.
So often I neglect him
I can't remember why.

Is he a tiny echo
Of other babes I've reared?
Or a fast-receding memory
Of youth that disappeared?

Bernie

Dreams of Berkshire

Berkshire County leaves me breathless
This heavenly vision in a valley.
From the top of the green rolling downs
To the meandering Thames and shallows
Fairest Berkshire most Royal County.
Here she stands in majestic splendour
Etched with leaves and branches arching
Held in lavish glowing colours
From the highest stone-built castle
To the humblest brick-built terrace.
It has all in fine profusion.
Just a glance and one must linger
Here England in its richest patchwork.
Holding all the finest stables
Where thoroughbreds are lively stepping
Athletes born of highest prowess
In most regal grandeur showing.
Shire filled with army's budding leaders
Old school ties, boaters, rowers
College pupils taught to perfection.
Scientific minds abound in measure
Glorious history in the making
The past now laid out in wonder.
Passing faces from times preceding
Catching at times unsuspecting
Place of warmth and childhood
It's you leads my heart ever homewards.

Colleen

If Only
Hindsight is such a wonderful gift
Think of the problems I could shift
If I knew then what I now know.
Life would be simple, correct and flow
Like a steady trickle of righteous bliss
Full of rewards that we all miss.

No more guilt, remorse or strife
The end of my troubles, a peaceful life...
But wait, is this the way to go
Days without regrets or woe?
I'd rather keep my naivety
Blunder along quite gleefully
Be glad I don't have all it takes
And proud to learn from my mistakes.

Tony Bennett

Question
Across the empty space
I saw the skull-like face
Bony arms hanging at his sides
His eyes open, vacant, wide.
Drawing in a chill deep breath
I smelled the smell of death.
I ran, running but moved no more
I tried to reach an open door.
Cold dank fog around me swirled
His bony fingers became unfurled.
I screamed and screamed in fear
As the skull came closer, near.
Suddenly warmth engulfed me once more.
I found the bedclothes on the floor.

Colleen Price

FAMILY & HOME

...where the heart is

The Berkshire Sound

Barksher born and Barksher bred
Strong in the arm and thick in the 'ed.
I be Barksher, I be buggery.
If I 'ad a bone, I'd naw 'im,
My wife 'ad 16 kids   (I'm a wife with)
An' I'm buggered if she (I) did'unt rear 'um

Very Very Old

The Birthday

I looked at my grandchildren's faces aglow with delight
A cake, shining with candles so bright.
There'd been laughter and shouting as each game was played
Excitement intense as the table was laid.
Then with wrappings all strewn and cards all read
So soon all quiet as they all trooped home to bed.

Colleen

Children

Children make me happy; children make me smile.
The problem is they're only children for a little while.
They grow up oh so quickly; they sprout like little trees.
It doesn't take too long before they're bashing on your knees.

Children are tiny versions of us and all we do
No matter how we deny it, this is a fact that's true.
You see it when they're sleeping and in their little eyes
And my God can you hear it – in their children's cries!

They are so very special because they're made with love
The joy they bring, the smiles they give feel like they're from above.
No matter what they do and no matter what they say
We know we'll always love them, in our own parental way.

We harvest them for nine months and nurture them for years
We wipe away their teardrops and erase all of their fears.
Wiping dirty bums while holding breath and heaving
Is something that we'll master and be so proud of achieving.

Just around the corner, lurk the teenage years
Of staying out and getting smashed on far too many beers.
So the moral of my poem is: enjoy it while you can
'cos pretty soon your baby'll be a woman or a man.

Chris Thomson

Ciara to Dad

I can't believe I am standing here today, saying my goodbyes.
To my dad who meant so much to me,
My Dad, with big brown eyes.

We'd have laughs and chats about nature, sun, moon and stars.
Anyone that knew my Dad will know the way I feel today,
For me he went way too fast.

So next time I look up at the skies
I know u'll be keeping an eye on me.
My Dad with big brown eyes
And ever ready smiles.

Love you Dad xxxxx

Ciara Lloyd Delaney

Cousins
Enveloped in loving friendship again
Memories rushing back.
Those eyes and smiles are still the same.

Oh! Sweet are the thoughts and words
The past is with us once more.
Stillness amongst the screaming hoards
Closeness more than the tie of blood.

Friendship's nearness
Not severed by the years and miles that could.
Words left unspoken, without word or deed
We know always
Our youthful hearts take heed.

Colleen

Cousin's Passing
Oh! Dick, the invisible one
Came and stole you from your chair
With the brush of an angel's wing
It was as if you'd never been there.
In that short space of time
Did your thoughts fly back to see
When we were young, you, Midge and me?
Did you meet all our loved ones
Who have passed away before?
Did they tell you we'd all laugh again
As we did in days of yore?
Keep all your memories tucked away, close
So once more we can share them
With those we love the most.

Colleen (2000)

Dad and Me

The morning's misty, very chill
We creep around not to awaken
Then flee away down river hill.
We find a place 'tween bank and brook
To bait and cast and wind and angle
Keeping very, very still.
The sun begins to shimmer slowly
Mist rolls away at last.
The river shines, slowly flowing.
Fish seem to need now, no company
So pack up gear, tramp back homeward.
Welcomed with hot toast and steaming mugs of tea.

Colleen

Daughter's Christmas

My daughter thinks of Christmas and something glows inside
With cheeks pinkly flushed and eyes glowing wide.
She thinks of parcels with ribbons and paper.
What can she get for each person later?
What can she plan now, for surprises
Can she wrap them in different disguises?
She plans and arranges all in whirl
Just as she did when she was a little girl.

Colleen

Elena Lucy

For that short sweet moment, I held her close
Her little body, soft and curved.
Her dark round eyes, my gaze she held
Her tiny fingers around mine curled.

My heart flipped with joy unbounded
As her little cry reached into my heart.
I caressed that smooth downy cheek
I was there to watch that new life start.

Memories of her mother's birth
I too hold close forever
Bringing clear again my daughter's warmth
Time will never sever.

As she is now, so once was I
Proud and ever guarding
Nothing in the world can change
Feelings of mother love rewarding.

Colleen 20/5/1996

Estranged Child

Rising like the tide beyond all control
Playing havoc with my thoughts, despair engulfs my soul.
Where is that stubborn pride for which I am renowned?
Eroded, crumbling to dust, soon to be scattered around
Like the sands of time, a distant memory within
Defeated in a battle it could never hope to win.

From where do they come these emotions full of pain?
Lying dormant, deceiving, daring to erupt again.
They destroy my contentment – allow no peace of mind
They attack my inner strength and leave a broken man behind.
What do they seek, these feelings, for what purpose did they rise
Gifted with such force yet containing no surprise?

For this attack is not the first by this cunning old foe
Recalled by my subconscious and allowed to grow and grow.
Yes, I must take the blame for my pitiful state
Willpower would assist my plight but alas it is too late.
Could there be a way to end this suffering inside
For these feelings of affection that have nowhere left to hide?

If only they could be released, allow my mind to rest
Yet someone dear to me could lift this burden from my chest.
For there is someone special, so respected and admired
The one who stole my heart and left me helpless and tired
Who only has to want me, then I will be free
Of these chains of emotion imprisoning me.
Until then I must endure a life of disarray
For I have so much love to give but she sends none my way.

Tony Bennett

Firstborn
Sitting playing dominoes
Trying to keep calm.
Not telling anyone
My baby was about to be born.

A taxi through a starry night
The coldness smelt of snow.
The very end of 1958
My whole being, all aglow.

Clocks far off striking midnight
Faintly cheering voices raised.
Recording every moment
I would remember all my days.

Snow now softly falling at the window
I felt my baby's kicking limbs.
Then she laid him in my arms
I looked so lovingly down at him.

Colleen

A Grandma, me?
A grandma, me? I never thought it would be.
Never thought my blood would descend
Thought it with my children would end.
Will there be a bond, will a friendship respond?

I want to feel those little hands entwine in mine
I want 'it' to know, I want to see 'it' grow.
I need to make it clear I shall always be near.
Will it be, as with mine, I'll read 'its' mind?
Will instinct and love make us hand in glove?

I never had a maternal gran'
She wasn't there to hold my hand.
I would dearly love to be
Just as I imagined her to be.

Colleen (1992 when told I was going to be a Grandma.)

Grandma and Grandads' Golden Wedding Anniversary

It's your 50th Anniversary
Represented by the colour of gold.
Even though you've reached it
You're still not so very old.

Gold is the colour of smiles
Gold is the colour of the sun
Gold is the colour of happiness
And knowing you are the only one.

Gold is the top of the mountain
On what is called the summit.
You have been climbing up all that time
Now you've both reached out and touched it.

Ellie Martin

If I Knew

(This reminds me of my mum on my last ever visit.)

If I knew it would be the last time
That I'd see you fall asleep,
I would tuck you in more tightly
And pray the Lord, your soul to keep.

If I knew it would be the last time
That I see you walk out the door,
I would give you a hug and kiss
And call you back for one more.

If I knew it would be the last time
I'd hear your voice lifted up in praise,
I would video-tape each action and word,
So I could play them back day after day.

If I knew it would be the last time,
I could spare an extra minute
To stop and say "I love you,"
Instead of assuming you would KNOW I do.

If I knew it would be the last time
I would be there to share your day,
Well I'm sure you'll have so many more,
So I can let just this one slip away.

For surely there's always tomorrow
To make up for an oversight,
And we always get a second chance
To make everything just right.

There will always be another day
To say "I love you,"
And certainly there's another chance
To say "Anything I can do?"

But just in case I might be wrong,
And today is all I get,
I'd like to say how much I love you
And I hope we never forget.

Tomorrow is not promised to anyone,
Young or old alike,
And today may be the last chance
You get to hold your loved one tight.

So if you're waiting for tomorrow,
Why not do it today?
For if tomorrow never comes,
You'll surely regret the day,

That you didn't take that extra time
For a smile, a hug, or a kiss
And you were too busy to grant someone,
What turned out to be their one last wish.

So hold your loved ones close today,
And whisper in their ear,
Tell them how much you love them
And that you'll always hold them dear.

Take time to say "I'm sorry,
Please forgive me, Thank you," or "It's okay."
And if tomorrow never comes,
You'll have no regrets about today.

Leslie Lobb

A father I had, this I know
He never acknowledged me though.
Before I was born
He took off in the dawn
He did not want a daughter – oh no!

This happened just after the War
In Birmingham district, Colmore.
Leslie Lobb was his name
A soldier his game.
He also played music galore.

A piano accordion had he
Every night in the pub on his knee.
I would so love to hear
From you, Daddy dear
Or your children related to me.

Bernie

Lewis James

I wasn't prepared for that feeling
As I held my grandson in my arms.
I didn't expect that 'proud feeling'
As I looked at his cherubic charms.

I saw nearly six pounds of wiggle
Dimples all around his face.
A surging love welled up through me
As the blood through my veins did race.

I gazed at him in wonder
And realized with breathtaking song
That somewhere in that tiny bundle
A little of me would go on and on.

Colleen 28/2/1993

Old Lady

See the old lady; she once had a son
Playing together for hours, full of fun.
She'd tell him stories, showing him games
Sorting his toys, giving them names.
Where is that young boy now you say?
He's with his family far away
With not a thought for those gentle hands
That soothed and rocked him in his pram.
She is too proud to shed a tear
To let anyone know she needs him here.

Anonymous

To Mum

Thank you for your sense of fun, those silly Irish jokes
Those Christmas gifts, those seaside trips, those stories of your folks.
Thank you for that fighting spirit, your will to overcome
Those wartime tales, that stubborn pride and drive to get things done.
Your shining path stays in our hearts to lead us on our way
Carved out despite life's cruellest blows to guide us should we stray.
As pain attacks and body breaks, as darkened days descend
Your constant faith from deep within, victorious till the end.
So now look down with pride and smile, and take a bow or two
For what you see and who we are is all because of you.

Tony Bennett

Sinead *(meaning 'Beloved of God')*
S is for Special – that's what you are
Intelligent too – you will be a star.
No-one can guess what you're thinking of

Everyone knows that you're easy to love.
Angels would queue for just one of your smiles.
Don't please ever grow too old for your wiles.

Auntie Bee

Tears of a Boy

Here's a boy with wild dark hair
Deep brown eyes that angry stare
Holding back the tears.
Little hero, you don't need
To grow with such alarming speed
Holding back the tears.

Life is hard for little boys
Taking all their simple joys
Giving back the tears.
You've been crying in your sleep
Only then the time to weep
Letting go the tears...

You'll never be a child again
Soon enough you'll be a man
And you won't need the tears.
I will help you all I can
In your race to be a man
I'll wipe away those tears.

But just remember when I'm gone
Heroes always soldier on.
Never needing tears.

Bernie (to a son)

Mother

Although she has no silken wings
Or halo made of gold

The love within her heart
Is all an angel heart could hold.
From my heart I say
A very loving prayer.
God bless you always
And keep you in His care.

Colleen W Price

Mother

God took the fragrance of a flower
The majesty of a tree
The gentleness of morning dew
The calm of a quiet sea
The beauty of a twilight hour
The soul of a starry night
The laughter of a rippling brook
The grace of a bird in flight.
Then God fashioned from these things
A creation like no other
And when His masterpiece was through
He called it simply...........MOTHER

Unknown

My Mum

Sweet are the memories of days gone by.
As you were then, so now am I
As you are now, I shall one day be.
Our time spins out for all to see
Our love goes on eternally

Colleen 1986 (Mum's 80th)

My Grandson

Give me your hand, oh grandson mine
Give me your smile, with your eyes a-shine.
I'll show a world full of wondrous things
Of sunshine and bees and birds on the wing.
We'll track through the forest and sail on a raft

Find haunted castles and ride a giraffe.
We'll make our own wings and fly through the skies.
Then we'll reach 'land of nod', singing sweet lullabies.
Colleen Feb 1994

Still Here

Some things are too deep for grief,
There's despair held in every leaf.
Will the sun never rise?
There's heaviness in black laden skies.
The child lays still and cold at her mother's breast
No warmth in the darkness of her new born crest.
Her journey has ended before it's begun
For her there'll be no childish fun.
Sobbing for a granddaughter we had but could not keep.
She weaves about my dreams as I sleep.
Colleen March 1995

My Treasure

My treasure they say, is just like me.
Cherub cheeks and eyes so knowing
Dark wispy curls, Oh! how she's growing.
My treasure they say
Is just like me.
Defiant gestures, lips a pouting.
Then shouts of glee, triumphant shouting.
My treasure they say
Is just like me.
Nervous wreck when marks are only 'seconds'
But shining eyes when history beckons.
My treasure they say
Is just like me
With blushing cheeks and lashes lowered
Not quite sure how compliments answered.
My treasure they say
Is just like me.
A working girl with serious passage
Try to improve the world.

My treasure they say
Is just like me
With the same hates and fancies.
All love of life and images dances.
My treasure they say
Is just like me.
A thought on wing, occurs twice over
Colours, shapes and forms, double discover.
My treasure they say
Is just like me.
As she puts her arms around me.
'Never leave me Mum,' says she.
My treasure they say
Is just like me
So on in time to be remembered
Closeness in thoughts never severed.

Colleen

Who is This Lady?

I had to meet a lady
Many years ago.
When I got to meet her
She smiled and said, "Hello."
I thought how kind and caring
As she got close to me
And sometimes used to tell me
About her memories.

Time went by, I married
(You'll never guess) her son
Who is the perfect father
To our own three currant buns.
Now that we are older
Things have sadly changed.
That lady turned from loving mum
To someone very strange.

I don't know who this woman is
She's really changed a lot.
Instead of being happy
She's content in being not.

I am in such a turmoil
Of how this came to be
It's playing on my mind
Just to think I cannot see.

One day she's fine
The next she's not
She says it's Family.
Surely if you've had nine kids
That's all the love you need.

I think she won't be happy
It's gone too far, you see.
From now on she'll be lonely
And unable to see
(like me).

Maddie Thomson

FOOD

Bon appetit

Beans, Beans, Beans

Baked beans,
Butter beans,
Big fat lima beans,
Long thin string beans—
Those are just a few.

Green beans,
Black beans,
Big fat kidney beans,
Red hot chilli beans,
Jumping beans too.

Pea beans,
Pinto beans,
Don't forget shelly beans.

Last of all,
Best of all,
I like jelly beans!
Kids101

Beefburgers

Take one pound of mince, very lean
Plus an onion, chopped finely and keen.
Stick these in a bowl
And mix them with soul
And a good pinch of herbs, nice and green.

Now add to your savoury mix
A handful of stuffing, real quick
Ketchup from a tube
A crumbled beef cube
Plus an egg, these delights to transfix.

Now shape your beef-burgers by hand
About six or so sounds very grand.
Just roll in a ball
Then flatten – that's all.
They're ready right now to be panned.

Or if you're a microwave star
Or would open a barbecue bar
Cook five minutes 'high'
And you'll decide why
You can kiss-bye McDonald's –Ta-rah!.

Bernie

Breakfast at 'The Royal'

Prince Charles and the Duchess of Cornwall are to make their Welsh farmhouse available as a holiday let...

A weekend off in rural Wales
An all-inclusive, off-peak fee
Now here at last, the two of us
Had booked the Royal B&B
With choice of white and wholegrain toasts
Or cereals on the dresser shelves
Amazed to see our regal hosts
At work on breakfast-shift themselves.

"Sleep well? Staying long?"
The Duchess smiled,
She, crisp of blouse
Doing 'front-of-house'
While in the kitchen, faintly-riled
At bain-marie, her aproned spouse.
"That's scrambled, Charles, and two fried slice!"
Camilla barked across the hall
"The eggs are free-range – fearf'ly nice.
They're 'By Appointment' after all."

Emboldened now and fortified
We asked if we'd see
Wills and Harry
"No," she chimed.
"We're out of tea,
I've sent them orf to Cash & Carry."
Martin Newell

Gravy

I'm a gravy monster
I like it quite a lot
On chips and chops and cabbage
So long as it is hot.

So don't serve me a dinner
That is dry and hard to swallow
Just pass the gravy boat pul-ease
And let me in it wallow.

Bernie

Peas

I eat my peas with honey,
I've done so all my life.
It makes my peas taste funny
But it keeps them on my knife.

Years old

Thanksgiving

'Twas the night of thanksgiving but I just couldn't sleep
I tried counting backwards, I tried counting sheep.
The leftovers beckoned – the dark meat and white
But I fought the temptation with all of my might.
Tossing and turning with anticipation
The thought of a snack became infatuation.
So I raced to the kitchen, flung open the door
And gazed at the fridge, full of goodies galore.
I gobbled up turkey and buttered potatoes,
Pickles and carrots, beans and tomatoes.
I felt myself swelling so plump and so round,
'Til all of a sudden, I rose off the ground.
I crashed through the ceiling, floating into the sky
With a mouthful of pudding and a handful of pie.
But, I managed to yell as I soared past the trees....
Happy eating to all – pass the cranberries, please.
May your stuffing be tasty, may your turkey be plump.
May your potatoes 'n gravy have nary a lump,
May your yams be delicious may your pies take the prize,
May your thanksgiving dinner stay off of your thighs.
Have a wonderful Thanksgiving!

Deb xx

IDEALS

The things we would most like to see or happen

Capital Punishment?

I do not think it civilised, or very just to boot
To simply hang, inject or gas these villains, or to shoot.
To murder those who've murdered is surely not the way.
It doesn't bring their victims back; it doesn't make them pay.
It surely doesn't compensate the families bereft
For once the murderer has gone – they'll still have nothing left.
And Life Imprisonment's a lie. The Law is such an ass!
Ten years or twenty isn't 'life' – it really is a farce.
No – killers should be made to pay by giving something back
Their quality of life perhaps to those who sadly lack.
I'd like to see them 'volunteered' for medical research
And all their worldly goods to go to charity or Church.
To lose their basic human rights would better suit the crime
Of homicide – the thing they stole – another person's time.

Bernie

Co-Existence

Peaceful co-existence seems to be a dirty word
Live and let live is now not assured.
Creatures, apart from humans, don't eliminate each other.
Then we have the gall to say, 'every man is my brother'.
We must stop this wicked torture and fearful lust
Put things to rights before it's too late and everything is dust.
Give back the land to all the creatures in desperate need
Give back the sea and replant the ravaged seed.

Colleen

English is so Hard

We'll begin with a box and the plural is boxes,
But the plural of ox should be oxen, not oxes.
Then one fowl is goose, but two are called geese,
Yet the plural of moose should never be meese.

You may find a lone mouse or a whole lot of mice,
But the plural of house is houses, not hice.
If the plural of man is always called men.
Why shouldn't the plural of pan be called pen.

The cow in the plural may be cows or kine,
But the plural of vow is vows, not vine.
And I speak of a foot and you show me your feet,
But I give you a boot – would a pair be called beet?

If one is a tooth and a whole set are teeth,
Why shouldn't the plural of booth be called beeth?
If the singular is this, and the plural is these,
Should the plural of kiss be named kese?

Then one may be that, and three may be those,
Yet the plural of hat would never be hose.
We speak of brother, and also the brethren,
But though we say mother, we never say methren.

The masculine pronouns are he, his and him,
But imagine the feminine she, shis and shim!
So our English, I think you will all agree,
Is the trickiest language you ever did see!

Anonymous

Festival of Remembrance

An exciting warmth wells up inside
As a sea of blue denim sways past.
Long hair, some straight, some curly
Then thunderous music and surging applause
The smell of Patchouli, wood fires and musk
Brings back nostalgic memories
Of Kaftans, flowers and beads at dusk.
Visions of peace and love, so sure
We could have changed the world.

Colleen

Innocence

Innocence, a fleeting thing
Like the blossoms of the spring
Like the pretty butterfly
Dancing now, but soon to die.
Not for long that wondering gaze
All too soon those baby days—
Are gone.

From 'Bobby's Girl'

Lament for England

Goodbye to my England, So long my old friend
Your days are numbered, being brought to an end
To be Scottish, Irish or Welsh that's fine
But don't say you're English, that's way out of line.

The French and the Germans may call themselves such
So may Norwegians, the Swedes and the Dutch
You can say you are Russian or maybe a Dane
But don't say you're English ever again.

At Broadcasting House the word is taboo
In Brussels it's scrapped, in Parliament too
Even schools are affected, staff do as they're told
They must not teach children about England of old.

Writers like Shakespeare, Milton and Shaw
The pupils don't learn about them anymore
How about Agincourt, Hastings , Arnhem or Mons ?
When England lost hosts of her very brave sons.

We are not Europeans, how can we be?
Europe is miles away over the sea
We're the English from England, let's all be proud
Stand up and be counted – Shout it out loud !

Let's tell our Government and Brussels too
We're proud of our heritage and the Red, White and Blue
Fly the flag of Saint George or the Union Jack
Let the world know – WE WANT OUR ENGLAND BACK !!!!

From The Queen's Royal Lancers

Morning

Sunrise across a shining brook
Primroses nestling in green moss
Minnows dancing in every nook
A PERFECT MORNING.

Let's not lose this lovely world
To chemicals and poisons
As our destruction readily unfurls
A SICKLY MORNING.

We'll fight on for a solution
Not use these killers.
Must put an end to this pollution
A DYING MORNING.

We'll spread the word of cure
Everyone must fight.
Get rid of choking evermore
A BRIGHT NEW MORNING.

Colleen

Painted Boy

A tear trickles
From the eye of a boy
Captured on canvas
Now sorrow for joy.
His eyes reflect sadness
Of Daddy's lost dreams
While clothes now in tatters
Rest upon seams.
His eyes never leave you
The stare never learns
Of life that drifts by him –
Life for which he yearned.

David Brewster

A Real Princess

It doesn't take a title
Nor money in the bank
It's not by education
Nor loads of pomp and swank.

If you are a Princess
You're nat'rul born that way
No powers nor peer pressures
Could ever make you sway.

It doesn't matter if your Daddy's rich
Or even if he's poor
If you are a REAL princess
You've natural allure.

You'll walk among your people
And all their hardships share.
You'll want to help so many
The problem's knowing where?

If you are REAL Princess
You'll know it in your heart.
You'll need to spread your sunshine
Such joy you will impart.

You'll walk your days in sunlight
And those you touch will share.
You'll bring your special glory
It's with you everywhere.

Diana was a REAL Princess

Her special gift was love.
She gave it all without reserve
'twas in her every move.

She'll never be forgotten
She'll be our Nation's Pride.
Like a jewel in our Crown
Her memory will bide.

Beautiful Diana
Within our hearts you reigned.
We may have lost our REAL Princess
But heaven an angel's gained.

Bernie

The Red Cross

The red cross on the white stands for England, so it ought.
To me it means St George and MY land — nowt to do with sport.
I'm not a football addict, nor even quite a fan
I hate the way it overtakes our telly and our man.
Yet, still I stop and think a mo' and wonder what I'm doing
Laden up with beers and pizzas; I'm a silly cow a-mooing.
And yet, and yet, I know it's good, it's some release or more
For mankind is competitive – surely sport is better than war?

Bernie

She is Gone

You can shed tears that she is gone,
Or you can smile because she has lived.
You can close your eyes and pray that she'll come back,
Or you can open your eyes and see all that she's left.
Your heart can be empty because you can't see her,
Or you can be full of the love you shared.
You can turn your back on tomorrow and live in yesterday,
Or you can be happy for tomorrow because of yesterday.
You can remember her and only that she's gone,
Or you can cherish her memory and let it live on.
You can cry and close your mind – be empty and turn your back,
Or you can do what she'd want: smile...
Open your eyes, love, and go on.
*Selected by the Queen to be read at the funeral of the Queen Mother
and many more besides - Anonymous*

Trog

I wish I lived in a cave
Life would be one big rave
Cool in the summer away from the sun
In winter I'd light a fire and have fun.

It's good to live in a cave
Think of the money you'd save
No electricity bills or phone
You could turn it into a lovely home.

We all should live in a cave
Especially those called Dave
Bring up your kids as Nature intended
No curtains to clean; no roof to be mended.

Our ancestors lived in a cave
And popped into the sea to bathe
Once a week they'd take a spear
And after the hunt they'd roast a deer.

Yes, I'm going to live in a cave
I'll have to be very brave
I'll change my middle name to Trog
Make do without a proper bog
And when I move into my cave
I won't even bother to shave.

My wife and kids will leave me for sure
I'll live the rest of my days so pure
Then I shall die in my cave
And it will become my grave.

Tony Bennett

Youth

Fire and thunder, peace and war
Pride and passion
Carnivore.

Blind rebellion, brimming rage
Dark frustration
Awkward age.

Understand him – blatant youth
Needing freedom
Seeking truth.

Dreams, ambitions, Nature's plan
Is what you're made of
Nearly Man.

Bernie

LIFE

...goes on

At Last

The sun is shining this morning
The rain at last has gone by.
The sun is shining this morning
There are traces of tear in my eye.
My heart stirs madly when remembering
I feel as though I'm going to die.
But the sun is shining this morning,
And I think that AT LAST I WON'T CRY.
Colleen 1990, 11years after Cancer all clear

Birthplace

Her eyes are moist; her hands atremble
As she gazes with memory's eye
At time that has swiftly been taken by.
Voices echo down that memory lane
Of sunshine, happiness, clouds and pain.
To see again this old familiar place
When her youth was lived apace.
Of laughter and tears still locked inside
As she now tells all with pride.
This is her roots; this is her birthright
And she has joyously won the fight.
Colleen

The Computer Swallowed Grandma

The computer swallowed grandma.
Yes, honestly it's true.
She pressed 'control' and 'enter'
And disappeared from view.

It devoured her completely;
The thought just makes me squirm.
She must have caught a virus
Or been eaten by a worm.

I've searched through the recycle bin
And files of every kind;
I've even used the Internet,
But nothing did I find.

In desperation, I asked Jeeves
My searches to refine.
The reply from him was negative,
Not a thing was found 'online'.

So, if inside your 'Inbox'
My Grandma you should see,
Please 'Copy', 'Scan' and 'Paste' her
And send her back to me!

Internet

County Corner

When Berkshire was a new born place
And sheep roamed in the fields
Reading Abbey was built by stone and flint
The bells of St Laurence pealed.

In Abingdon the Abbot sang
When the county was but new.
The Abbey grew bigger year by year
And the town around it grew.

Wallingford Castle, now razed to the ground
Is left for children's play.
Now malt invades the local air
And steam engines are back to stay.

In Newbury they went milling flour
The farmers raising sheep.
On the Kennet and Avon barges came
Unlucky few to Coombe Gibbet steep.

At Windsor the Castle stands supreme
Our reigning monarch's home.
Famous gardens about it, in bloom
And Henry the eighth's deer still roam.

In Reading, Huntley and Palmer's biscuits baked
And Sutton's seeds were sown.
The smell of Simond's beer invaded the town
But now state of the art has grown.

Villages and Towns around Berkshire lie
With their churches, schools and greens.
May nothing ever change their ways
Let them stay as in our dreams.

Colleen 1980

Crabby Old Man

What do you see nurses? What do you see?
What are you thinking when you're looking at me?
A crabby old man, not very wise,
Uncertain of habit with faraway eyes?
Who dribbles his food and makes no reply.
When you say in a loud voice "I do wish you'd try!"
Who seems not to notice the things that you do.
And forever is losing a sock or a shoe?
Who, resisting or not lets you do as you will,
With bathing and feeding. The long day to fill?
Is that what you're thinking? Is that what you see?
Then open your eyes, nurse – you're not looking at me.

I'll tell you who I am as I sit here so still,
As I do all at your bidding, and I eat at your will.
I'm a small child of ten with a father and mother,
Brothers and sisters who love one another
A young boy of sixteen with wings on his feet
Dreaming that soon now a lover he'll meet.
A groom soon at twenty; my heart gives a leap.
Remembering the vows that I promised to keep.
At twenty-five, now I have young of my own
Who need me to guide – and a secure happy home.

A man of thirty my young now grown fast,
Bound to each other with ties that should last.
At forty, my young sons have grown and are gone,
But my woman's beside me to see I don't mourn.
At fifty, once more, babies play 'round my knee,
Again, we know children my loved one and me.

Dark days are upon me. My wife is now dead.
I look at the future; I shudder with dread.
For my young are all rearing young of their own
And I think of the years and the love that I've known.
I'm now an old man and nature is cruel.
'Tis jest to make old age look like a fool.
The body, it crumbles; grace and vigour depart.
There is now a stone where I once had a heart.
But inside this old carcass a young man still dwells,
And now and again my battered heart swells
I remember the joys; I remember the pain.
And I'm loving and living life over again.
I think of the years – all too few – gone too fast.
And accept the stark fact that nothing can last. So open your eyes, people
Open and see.
Not a crabby old man: Look closer. SEE........ME!!

Anonymous

Days Gone By

Heartfelt thoughts of days gone by
When we were young, you and I.
The animals and trees, the birds and bees
Each year blossoming again as new.
Where has it gone, why destroyed
Where once there was peace and love?
No time now for olive branch and dove.
We've killed, poisoned and wiped out
What living and loving was all about.
It's not too late to alter now all we've ignored
Then we'd see again, the blessings of the Lord.

Colleen

Divorce

She paid rapt attention to the carpet design
He did the same to his pint of beer.
She wished she were ten thousand miles away
He just wished she were here.

He smoked a rolled-up cigarette
She smoked a brand that was strong,
As she dreamily savoured her newly-won life,
While he wondered how things had gotten so wrong.

She whispered the words of an old favourite song
He joined – mistaking her meaning.
She shed a few reminiscent tears
He carried on – wildly dreaming.

He reached for her hand.
She snatched it away,
Brushing invisible specks from her lap
Then she endeavoured to say...

"I don't understand why you keep up this farce
Why can't you see there's no way?
I cannot revive what has long since died
There's nothing more I can say."

He cried like a baby;
He pleaded and begged her to stay.
She hated herself like a louse
But still she got up – and walked away.

Bernie

Driftwood

Half my life ago
I played here when young.
Now it is so empty;
The memory too strong.
But still it seems
Like only yesterday
That the sand between our toes
Used to drift away
To the scattered sand dunes,
Too far to even see.
And your ghost it still belongs here.
I walk within a dream
Of when we laughed as children.
Now time is a demand –
The time we had so long ago
Like driftwood on the sand.

Dave Brewster

The End

With mixture of relief and fear
The dreaded day at last was here.
Would they find out what was wrong
Would I have the strength to carry on?

Then the fearful words uttered low
'The dreaded killer's begun to grow',
With aching heart and sad surprise,
Hot tears welling from my eyes.

Never to see my family grow,
Any grandchild I'd never know.
When I go with deep regret,
Will they very soon forget?

Will it really be, I once was here?
Will my face still be very dear?
Or will it all so swiftly fade?
As I take my heartache to my grave.

Colleen 1979

Entertainment?

Murder, mystery
Suspense and crime
To thrill the young
Before bedtime.
While the adults
Up till dawn
Hear a poem of love
And yawn.

Dave Brewster

The Experiment

Way back in the dawn of time
We crawled out from all that slime
Took this world with fire and words
Took it from the beasts and birds.
Took this world and made it pay
Thought we'd run it *our* way.

No more jungles in the mist
Flint and bronze and iron fist.
Concrete cities rise from dust
Swords then guns, machines then rust.
No more fishes in the sea
Gone to nourish you and me.

No more herds of buffalo
Their land's gone to reap and sow.
No more monkeys in the trees
Their wood's gone to factories.

Disease, pollution, pain and war
We brought this world our ancient scar.
Where we came from, who can tell?
Alpha, space or Mars or hell.
Now we reach out to the stars
If we make it they'll be ours.
But if we blow ourselves to hell
This fair world will go as well.
If we fail before our time,
We'll crawl back to all that slime.

Bernie

Ghost Dance

May the stars carry your sadness away,
May the flowers fill your heart with beauty,
May hope forever wipe away your tears,
And, above all, may silence make you strong.

~ Chief Dan George ~

The Gift of Laughter

Cultivate a sense of humour;
Let your heart be gay.
Send a glimpse of welcome sunshine
Through the dullest day.

See the funny side of things
At times of your expense;
Surely to dispel the gloom
Is ample recompense.

Put aside that brooding sorrow;
Watch concern and cares grow less.
Lift your face towards tomorrow;
Lift your heart to happiness.

Ellen Bennett

Hands

Little tiny cherub fingers, gripping at the lacy shawl
Growing noisily into boyhood
Cut and bruised in schoolyard brawl.
Now nervous tension gripping tightly.

Endless papers written scrawl.
Free now of repressing forces
Beginning to be a man.
FEELING LOVE, HATE AND LONGING
Wanting to give all he can.

Suddenly a rifle butt pressed in them
Learn to maim, learn to kill.
Warm strong hands turn cold and rigid
Lay palm upwards very still.

Colleen

Leisure

What is this life if, full of care,
We have no time to stand and stare?
No time to stand beneath the boughs
And stare as long as sheep or cows:
No time to see, when woods we pass,
Where squirrels hide their nuts in grass:
No time to see, in broad daylight,
Streams full of stars, like skies at night:
No time to turn at Beauty's glance,
And watch her feet, how they can dance:
No time to wait till her mouth can
Enrich that smile her eyes began?
A poor life this, if full of care,
We have no time to stand and stare.

William Henry Davies b.1871

Man

I know my soul hath power to know all things,
Yet she is blind and ignorant in all.
I know I'm one of Nature's little kings,
Yet to the least and vilest things am thrall.

I know my life's a pain and but a span;
I know my sense is mock'd in everything;
And to conclude, I know myself a Man –
Which is a proud and yet a wretched thing.

Sir John Davies (1569-1626)

Memories

A little house with three bedrooms
And one car on the street,
A mower that you had to push
To make the grass look neat.

In the kitchen on the wall
We only had one phone,
And no need for recording things,
Someone was always home.

We only had a living room
Where we would congregate,
Unless it was at mealtime
In the kitchen where we ate.

We had no need for family rooms
Or extra rooms to dine,
When meeting as a family
Those two rooms would work out fine.

We only had one TV set,
And channels maybe two,
But always there was one of them
With something worth the view.

For snacks we had potato chips
That tasted like a chip,
And if you wanted flavor
There was Lipton's onion dip.

Store-bought snacks were rare
Because my mother liked to cook,
And nothing can compare
To snacks in Betty Crocker's book.

Weekends were for family trips
Or staying home to play,
We all did things together –
Even go to church/synagogue to pray.

When we did our weekend trips,
Depending on the weather,
No one stayed at home
Because we liked to be together.

Sometimes we would separate
To do things on our own,
But we knew where the others were
Without our own cell phone.

Then there were the movies
With your favorite movie star,
And nothing can compare to
Watching movies in your car.

Then there were the picnics at
The peak of summer season,
Pack a lunch and find some trees
And never need a reason.
(notice how we dressed!)

Get a baseball game together
With all the friends you know.
Have real action playing ball –
And no game video.

Remember when the doctor
Used to be the family friend,
And didn't need insurance
Or a lawyer to defend?

The way that he took care of you
Was what he had to do,
Because he took an oath and
Strived to do the best for you.
(and sometimes that meant coming to your home)

Remember going to the store
And shopping casually,
And when you went to pay for it
You used your own money?

Nothing that you had to swipe
Or punch in some amount.
Remember when the cashier person
Had to really count?
(Why I think they even knew the name of everyone on every bill)

The milkman used to go
From door to door,
And it was just a few cents more
Than going to the store.

There was a time when mailed
Letters came right to your door,
Without a lot of junk mail ads
Sent out by every store.

The mailman knew each house by name
And knew where it was sent;
There were not loads of mail
Addressed to "present occupant".

There was a time when just one glance
Was all that it would take,
And you would know the kind of car,
The model and the make.

They didn't look like turtles
Trying to squeeze out every mile;
They were streamlined, white walls, fins,
And really had some style.

One time the music that you played
Whenever you would jive,
Was from a vinyl, big-holed record
Called a forty-five.

The record player had a post
To keep them all in line,
And then the records would drop down
And play one at a time.

Oh sure, we had our problems then,
Just like we do today,
And always we were striving,
Trying for a better way.

Oh, the simple life we lived
Still seems like so much fun,
How can you explain a game,
Just kick the can and run?

And why would boys put baseball cards
Between bicycle spokes,
And for a nickel red machines
Had little bottled Cokes?

This life seemed so much easier
And slower in some ways,
I love the new technology
But I sure do miss those days.

So time moves on and so do we,
And nothing stays the same,
But I sure love to reminisce
And walk down memory lane.

An American child of the Sixties

Memory

So shuts the marigold her leaves
At the departure of the sun;
So from the honeysuckle sheaves
The bee goes when the day is done;
So sits the turtle when she is but one,
And so all woe, as I since she is gone.

To some few birds kind Nature hath
Made all the summer as one day:
Which once enjoy'd, cold winter's wrath
As night they sleeping pass away.
Those happy creatures are, that know not yet,
The pain to be deprived or to forget.

I oft have heard men say there be
Some that with confidence profess
The helpful Art of Memory:
But could they teach Forgetfulness?
I'd learn; and try what further art could do
To make me love her and forget her too.

William Browne (1588-1643)

Not Seeing is Believing

I do not see the trees so strong
But I feel their strength.
I do not see the birds on wing
But I hear them sing.

The beautiful flowers in springtime, I do not see
But their perfume fills my head.
They bring so much joy to me.

The children playing in the lane

Call to me and speak my name.
Friends come in to wish me well;
They have many a tale to tell.

The changing seasons come and go; this I know.
But always there is a helping hand
To guide me through the snow.

As darkness falls and lights come on,
I go inside and close the door.
Soon the friendly policeman calls
To say goodnight once more.

And you my wonderful four-legged friend.
Will be my eyes until the end.

Margaret J. Robinson (a blind lady)

Pollution

A dust bowl of remembrance
As things as were before
Of trees , vines and undergrowth
From treetop, to the floor.
Where myriads of insects and every living thing
Was once so very commonplace
And all the birds did sing.
Now all that lies forgotten
The only thing that's left
Is struggling man, existing
A skeletal death.

Colleen

Reading lifetime

Reading was waiting for me
Its arms around me curled.
I snuggled up, trusting
I said 'hello' to the world.

I knew my home was timeless
As I learned to talk.
I was forever learning
As the roads and lanes I walked.

With ration books and gasmasks
And the will to win
Queuing for Mum in food shops
And aching in every limb.

War was over; we lived again.
Growing up to adulthood
With Teddy Boys and 78s
The rock and roll was good.

A wedding very soon took place
All this was surely meant to be.
In time my children too were born
Love still strong for all to see.

One time I nearly didn't make it
But I was given another chance.
Again Reading's arms were around me
Every moment was enhanced.

Many times I could have left here
But the pull was far too strong.
This friendship goes on forever,
My Reading life goes on.

Colleen 1992

Not Really

I smile but I don't really see you
To me you are not really there.
You talk but I don't really hear you
My mind is adrift on the air.

I eat without really tasting
I touch but I don't really feel.
I dream but I don't believe it
I know that illusion too well.

I work but I don't really notice
It's hard but I don't really care.
My hands do the things they're supposed to
My mind has flown off somewhere.

I laugh when I know it is pleasing
I act and I play my part.
I cry without really easing
The loneliness in my heart.

Bernie (1981-8 as a factory worker).

Relief

The grass and trees are green again
Mist has lifted from my eyes.
Tears of relief are flowing down
No more heartfelt sighs.
The test was normal this time they said
My heart with lightness soars.
To be part of life again,
Peace will come once more.

Colleen

Retirement

I worked years for someone else so that I could retire.
I dreamed of sleeping late and sitting by the fire.
I dreamed of long vacations, enjoying stage and song.
But, let me set you straight on that concept,
It is simply wrong.
I did junk my safety glasses
And the work boots that cramped my toes.
But the rest of it had a mind of its own and this is how it goes.
My wife had been thinking of retirement
And had plans of her own.
She had spent much time with the kids but now they are grown and gone.
We sold our cattle and horses so we wouldn't have that chore.
I poured concrete over my alarm clock but I still wake up at four.
I get my eyes checked on Monday.
Ann gets hers checked the next day.
I go for a colon check on Wednesday and pass my wife going the other way.
I have a dental appointment on Thursday.
Ann goes for a test on her heart.
Friday we go get prescriptions filled and browse a while at Walmart.
Saturdays we just stay home and try to get the paperwork right.
We can't take any overnight trips
'Cause we can't see to drive at night.
Restroom confusion keeps us out of church on Sunday
And we really do hate that.
There's nothing wrong with the restrooms,
We just can't remember where they're at.
We don't need to plan next week, just make sure we can drive.
And not forget where the hospitals and clinics are.
We'll need them to survive.
So, don't build your castles too high, my friend,
While strolling through the clover.
This is a typical week in retirement and on Monday we start over!

Anonymous

Right?

Is it right to look at life in black and white
Or should it be the way
To look at it with a touch of grey
As when bad laws are passed
And our freedoms are put last
Should we not ask
Or take them to task?
And now education has been put to bed
It's now a crime to phone while looking ahead
encouraging people to look down and text.
They invent laws without thinking what will be next.
Three points and a thirty pound fine
They won't be happy till they have my last dime.
Smoking and driving is now a crime
They won't be happy till we all stand in line.
The parties yellow, blue and red
Won't be happy till I'm dead.
They want us all never to blink;
They hate people who like to think.
Yes it scares me and I'm not alone;
Their schedule is to make me a clone
to stand in line where they want me to be
instead of speaking out and being free.
Is it right to look at life in black and white
Or should it be the way
To look at it with a touch of grey?
This is not the country I once knew
When it was legal to speak one's view.
Now we are told what we must lose
And not be allowed to pick and choose.
In memory of all those who have died
All in vain now it feels from inside.
The PC brigade are a growing bunch
While they plot what to do next over their tax-free lunch.

Colin (on MySpace)

Rock that Cradle

The men of tomorrow
Are babes in arms today.
The very arms that hold them
Must surely hold the key.

Yes, Mother – the power is yours
And always has been so
To make these future people
To watch them learn and grow.

You've done a lousy job so far
Just look around and see
That war and poverty and crime
Were learned at Mother's knee.

So Mother, pull your socks up
And take time to be told:
The men of tomorrow
Are yours to shape and mould.

Bernie

Ships that Pass

Ships that pass in the night and greet each other in passing;
Only a signal shown and a distant voice in the darkness.
So, on the ocean of life we pass and greet one another;
Only a look, a voice, then darkness again and silence.

Beatrice Harraden (1864-1936)

Slow Dance

Have you ever watched kids
On a merry-go-round?
Or listened to the rain
Slapping on the ground?

Ever followed a butterfly's erratic flight?
Or gazed at the sun into the fading night?
You better slow down.
Don't dance so fast.
Time is short.
The music won't last.

Do you run through each day
On the fly?
When you ask 'How are you?'
Do you hear the reply?
When the day is done
Do you lie in your bed
With the next hundred chores
Running through your head?

You'd better slow down
Don't dance so fast.
Time is short.
The music won't last.

Ever told your child,
We'll do it tomorrow?
And in your haste,
Not see his sorrow?
Ever lost touch,
Let a good friendship die
'Cause you never had time
To call and say, 'Hi'

You'd better slow down.
Don't dance so fast.
Time is short.
The music won't last.

When you run so fast to get somewhere
You miss half the fun
Of getting there
When you worry and hurry through your day,
It is like an unopened gift...
Thrown away.

Life is not a race.
Do take it slower
Hear the music
Before the song is over.

Anonymous

Some People

I look around through the sunshine and rain.
I see happy people; I see people with pain,
Bright lights and bright clothes:
Some of them are lonely.
How many? God knows!

I look around the precincts and pavements.
Some of the people look hungry;
Some want judgement to take them.
It's a fast life with high finance
Money is the new romance.
Too bad if you're ugly.

I've looked around government places;
Some people have no hope on their faces.
Some are called problems;
Some are called 'born to lose'
But all of them are numbers now,
More paperwork to peruse.

I look at the hatred in people's eyes.
Some have fun by kicking heads;
Some don't care for life.
Some will use you; most want power –
Power to escape the frustration
Of a thing called civilization.

I've looked around a while;
I think it's a crying shame
So many people crying in vain,
And how many? God knows!

Dave Brewster

Train Wheels

A far off train thundering down the track takes me back
To a time when I was fresh and young
Wondering, about the things to come.
Now I'm old and time has gone
Worn and weary now; life has taken
All I could give and now forsaken.

I would love to stand once more
Near that 'old days' track and hear *that* engine's roar!
I would do again the things I've left undone
Undo the things I should *not* have done.
But we never get a second chance.
We only have one whirling dance.

Colleen

Wasted Moments

What is this life of misspent summers?
No thought to hurt, when hearts are young
The pain of word and deed unthinking
The things left still and songs unsung.
Wasted moments, missing chances
No speculation of future years.
A backward glance of youth enhances
No place for heartache and painful tears
A hardness now built within him.
No feeling of soft warmth, nearness
Steely eyes that hearts can't win.
Turn away cold, rejecting closeness.

Colleen

What is Life?

And what is Life? An hour-glass on the run,
A mist retreating from the morning sun,
A busy, bustling, still-repeated dream.
Its length? A minute's pause, a moment's thought.
And Happiness? A bubble on the stream,
That in the act of seizing shrinks to nought.

And what is Hope? The puffing gale of morn,
That of its charms divests the dewy lawn,
And robs each flow'ret of its gem – and dies;
A cobweb, hiding disappointment's thorn,
Which stings more keenly through the thin disguise.

And what is Death? Is still the cause unfound?
That dark mysterious name of horrid sound?
A long and lingering sleep the weary crave.
And Peace? Where can its happiness abound?
Nowhere at all, save heaven and the grave.

Then what is Life? When stripped of its disguise,
A thing to be desired it cannot be;
Since everything that meets our foolish eyes
Gives proof sufficient of its vanity.
'Tis but a trial all must undergo,
To teach unthankful mortals how to prize
That happiness vain man's denied to know,
Until he's called to claim it in the skies.

John Clare

When We Were Children

Just remembering times gone by
When we were children you and I.
All the things we said and did
Grown-ups thought, we were 'just a kid'.
Long remembered, silly days
That rolling onward, changed our ways.
But deep down, we are as then
And we can relive those times again.

Colleen

A Woman's Poem

He didn't like the casserole
And he didn't like my cake.
My biscuits were too hard
Not like his mother used to make.

I didn't perk the coffee right
He didn't like the stew
I didn't mend his socks
The way his mother used to do.

I pondered for an answer
I was looking for a clue.
Then I turned around and smacked him
Like his Mother used to do.

Anonymous

LOVE

...makes the world go round

Annabel

I bow my head; the hot tears flow
The rest of me is numb.
I lift my eyes to leaden skies
But they don't see the sun.

Despair is etched in every line
Sorrow floods my face.
I hold out my arms for comfort
But there is no embrace.

The wind has dropped; the trees are still
Not a leaf now stirs.
I look into my daughter's eyes
And see the misery is hers.

I act, I talk, I play my part
The front is just for show.
The death of my grand-daughter
Has left a void no one can know.

She holds the child against her breast
There's no movement to perceive
It's all over now
Nothing now but to grieve.

Colleen

Around the Corner

Around the corner I have a friend
In this great city that has no end
Yet the days go by and weeks rush on
And before I know it, a year is gone.
And I never see my old friend's face
For life is a swift and terrible race.
He knows I like him just as well
As in the days when I rang his bell
And he rang mine, but we were younger then
And now we are busy, tired men.
Tired of playing a foolish game
Tired of trying to make a name.
"Tomorrow" I say "I will call on Jim
Just to show that I'm thinking of him."
But tomorrow comes and tomorrow goes
And distance between us grows and grows.
Around the corner, yet miles away,
"Here's a telegram sir. Jim died today."
And that's what we get and deserve in the end
Around the corner, a vanished friend.

Anonymous

Believe

I believe in miracles and dreams that will come true.
I believe in tender moments and friendship, through and through.
I believe in stardust and moonbeams all aglow.
I believe there is magic and more there than we know.

I believe in reaching out and touching from the heart.
I believe that if we touch a gift we can impart.
I believe that if you cry your tears are not in vain.
And when you are sad and lonely, others know your pain.

I believe that when we laugh a sparkle starts to shine.
And I just know that spark will spread from more hearts than just
mine.
I believe that hidden in the quiet of the night,
There is magic, moths and gypsies, a fairy and a sprite.

I believe that if you dance the dances of your heart,
That greater happiness will find a brand new way to start.
I believe the gifts you have are there for you to share
And when you give them from the heart, the whole world knows you
care.

I believe that if you give, even just to one,
That gift will grow in magnitude before the day is done.
I believe that comfort comes from giving part of me.
And if I share with others, there is more for all to see.

I believe that love is still the greatest gift of all
And when it's given from the heart the gift is never small.

Anonymous

To Celia

Drink to me only with thine eyes
And I will pledge with mine
Or leave a kiss but in the cup
And I'll not look for wine.
The thirst that from the soul doth rise
Doth ask a drink divine
But might I of Jove's nectar sup
I would not change for thine.

I sent thee late a rosy wreath
Not so much honouring thee
As giving it a hope that there
It could not wither'd be
But thou thereon didst only breathe
And sent'st it back to me
Since when it grown, and smells, I swear,
Not of itself but thee!

Ben Jonson (1573-1637)

E-friends

I've a warm and friendly feeling
As I think of you today
And I wish that we could visit
But you're many miles away.

Separated by such distance,
Yet your emails bring you near
Through the miles we share a friendship
That's become to me most dear.

Friends through correspondence only
Still, your face I need not see
For your soul shines through the pages
Every time you write to me.

You've a special way of writing
Warming as the sunshine rays
Bringing joy and inspiration
Letter brightening up my days.

You've enriched my life, my dear one
And I'm glad God willed we meet
"Friendship's Road" is that much nicer
Travelling it with one so sweet.

from Deb xx

An English Love Poem

Of course I love ya darling
You're a bloody top notch bird
And when I say you're gorgeous
I mean every single word
So ya bum is on the big side
I don't mind a bit of flab
It means that when I'm ready
There's somethin' there to grab
So your belly isn't flat no more
I tell ya, I don't care
So long as when I cuddle ya
I can get my arms round there
No woman who is your age
Has nice round perky breasts
They just gave in to gravity
But I know ya did ya best
I'm tellin ya the truth now
I never tell ya lies

I think it's very sexy
That you've got dimples on ya thighs
I swear on me grannie's grave now
The moment that we met
I thought you was as good as
I was ever gonna get
No matter wot you look like
I'll always love ya dear
Now shut up while the football's on
And fetch another beer.

Internet

Friend

She's the reason behind my sense
She is the grass beyond my fence.
She brings me up; she brings me down
And promises she'll be around.
She takes away all of my fears
So all my darkness disappears.
She wakes me up, brings me around
Sends all my demons crashing down.
She is the candle in my night
I know with her there'll be no fight.
She lifts me up; I know I've found
A friend I know will be around.
She might be strange but so am I
Without each other our rarity would die.
She shakes me up; she turns me round
Lifting me to higher ground.
I'll end this note one thing to say
I hope I'll never see the day.
She flies and leaves no longer two
No life I'd have without the friend – that's you
Friend.

Chris Thomson

Goodbye

Goodbye my dear
Our paths divide
For so it has to be
We cannot walk together on the road to destiny.
I know that now
And although I will always treasure in my heart
The things that could or might have been
The time has come to part.

Jacqueline Fleur Patey

Month to Marry

January – Marry when the year is new, he'll be loving, kind and true.

February – When February birds do mate, you wed nor dread your fate.

March – If you wed when March winds blow, joy and sorrow both you'll know.

April – Marry in April if you can; joy for maiden and for man.

May – Marry in the month of May; you will romance the day.

June – Marry when June roses grow and over land and sea you'll go.

July – Those who in July do wed must labour for their daily bread.

August – Whoever wed in August be, many a change is sure to see.

September – Marry in September's shine so that your life is rich and fine.

October – If in October you do marry, love will come but riches tarry.

November – If you wed in bleak November, only joys will come, remember!

December – When December's snows fall fast, marry and your love will last.

Anonymous

If I Could Catch a Rainbow

I would do it just for you
And share with you its beauty
On the days you're feeling blue.

If I could build a mountain
You could call your very own;
A place to find serenity,
A place to be alone.

If I could take your troubles
I would toss them in the sea,
But all these things I'm finding
Are impossible for me.

I cannot build a mountain
Or catch a rainbow fair,
But let me be what I know best,
A friend who's always there.

Internet

Recovery

The time has come for tears to start again
Those faithful tears that always ease the pain.
Release the raging rivers of my soul!
Let me drown and then rise up again.

Let me drown until the river dries
Until the numbing coldness settles in
See the world once more with empty eyes
No spark of warmth can penetrate the skin.

Crash the thunder! Howl the wind!
Freeze my heart and beat the driving rain!
Let me know these dreams are empty lies
Let me die and come to life again.

In the silent darkness of my mind
Let me wonder who you really are.
Let me feel that you were just a dream
That fades on waking like the morning star.

From 'Bobby's Girl'

Sent

Where are they now – those friends of mine
Those blissful days of yore?
With laughs and tears and *Auld Lang Sine*
Those wireless, records, and gramophones.
Dressed in whirling skirts and sloppy joes
Boys in Teddy suits and greasy combs
Thick suede creepers, stamping on our toes.
We thought we were 'it' and 'the end'.
In circle-stitched cups, paper nylon slips
We danced away, friend to friend.
A bar of music, a snatch of song,
I relive those moments and pretend.

Colleen

Silver Wedding

A Silver Wedding – Aren't you proud?
You should stand out among the crowd.
Not many stand the test of years
But you two are the BEST, my dears.

Ellen Bennett (to her daughter, Lyz and hubby on their silver wedding anniversary).

Sin?
They say it is a sin to love
The reason I know not why
But I will sin by loving you until the day I die.

Jacqueline Fleur Patey

Stop All the Clocks, Cut off the Telephone

Stop all the clocks, cut off the telephone,
Prevent the dog from barking with a juicy bone.
Silence the pianos and with muffled drum
Bring out the coffin, let the mourners come.

Let aeroplanes circle, moaning overhead
Scribbling on the sky the message: He Is Dead.
Put the crepe bows round the white necks of the public doves
Let the traffic policemen wear black cotton gloves.

He was my North, my South, my East and West,
My working week and my Sunday's rest,
My noon, my midnight, my talk, my song;
I thought that love would last forever: I was wrong.

The stars are not wanted now: put out every one.
Pack up the moon and dismantle the sun;
Pour away the ocean and sweep up the wood.
For nothing now can ever come to any good.

W.H. Auden

Wedding Anniversaries

The 1st is PAPER, on which you can write
The 2nd is COTTON, all crisp and white,
The 3rd is LEATHER, a bag or some gloves,
The 4th is BOOKS, Lady Chatterley's loves!
The 5th is WOOD, a box full of dreams,
The 6th is IRON, metal not steam
The 7th is WOOL, soft and warm
The 8th is BRONZE, metal in an elegant form
The 9th is COPPER, and 10th is TIN,
If you have got this far you are bound to win.
The 11th is STEEL, so shiny and bright
The 12th is SILK, so soft and so light,

The 13th is LACE, maybe a cloth for a tray,
The 14th is IVORY, leave it for Jumbo,
It's better that way!
The 15th is CRYSTAL, cut glass at its best,
The 20th CHINA, cups, plates and the rest,
The 25th is SILVER – really swell
The 30th is PEARL – from an oyster's shell
The 35th is CORAL, from under the sea
The 40th is RUBY, as red as red can be
The 45th is SAPPHIRE – precious and blue
The 50th is GOLDEN – Congratulations to you!
The 55th is EMERALD – so green and so pure,
The 60th DIAMOND – an achievement for sure.
The 65th BLUE SAPPHIRE, and 70th PLATINUM
The last two which are reached by some
The 75th is DIAMOND AND GOLD
The 80th OAK
Or something suitable for the very old!

Internet

Wedding Message

Sent to Jim and Paulis on their Wedding day
Let all of your rainbows divulge pots of gold.
May you never go grey until you are old.
Let your joys be abundant
And troubles far few
May you never forget
To say 'I love you'

Bernie

Young Love

Suddenly seen that old familiar face
Quickens the heart, the pulses race.
The feel of those strong hands once more
Bring love and memories flooding back.

The years roll away, tears sting the eyes
Once more seventeen, soft teenage sighs.
This wonderful love is full and strong
And will last deeply on and on.

No more peace and contentment fill my heart
I'm torn apart, such sweet pain
Must I live through this all again?

The love I thought I'd cloaked
Now comes pouring from my throat.
Please give me strength to survive
A lasting love I can only hide.

Colleen

MYTH & MAGIC

Say the magic words

A Sheepish Fairy-tale

Bronwyn was a little sheep
Her fleece was white as snow
And everything she saw and heard
She always had to know.

One day she found a nice clear pond
And didn't need a bath.
She thought she'd try the 'magic mirror'
Theory for a laugh.

"Oh magic water, clear and deep,
Who is the fairest of all sheep?"

Bert Ram hid behind a bush
And sniggered as he thought
Then spoke in deep and booming voice
Which Bronwyn quickly bought.

"Over seven jewelled hills
And seven meadows too,
I have found none fairer
The fairest sheep is ewe."

Bernie

Dragon Song

Once there was a dragon, dressed in green,
Dressed in green, all in green.
Never has a worse one yet been seen
Than the dragon who was dressed in green.
Envious and Spiteful is his name, dreadful name, dragon's name
Envious and Spiteful is his name,
The dragon who is dressed in green.
Should you ever meet him, some fine day, some fine day, far away...
Should you ever meet him, you must SLAY
The dragon who is dressed in green.

Song learned c.1954. (Don't try this at home.)

The Fairies

Up the airy mountain,
Down the rushy glen,
We daren't go a-hunting
For fear of little men;
Wee folk, good folk,
Trooping all together;
Green jacket, red cap,
And white owl's feather!

Down along the rocky shore
Some make their home,
They live on crispy pancakes
Of yellow tide foam;
Some in the reeds
Of the black mountain lake,
With frogs for their watch-dogs,
All night awake.

High on the hill-top
The old King sits;
He is now so old and gray
He's nigh lost his wits.
With a bridge of white mist
Columbkill he crosses,
On his stately journeys
From Slieveleague to Rosses;
Or going up with music
On cold starry nights
To sup with the Queen
Of the gay Northern Lights.

They stole little Bridget
For seven years long;
When she came down again
Her friends were all gone.
They took her lightly back,
Between the night and morrow,
They thought that she was fast asleep,
But she was dead with sorrow.
They have kept her ever since
Deep within the lake,
On a bed of flag-leaves,
Watching till she wake.

By the craggy hill-side,
Through the mosses bare,
They have planted thorn trees
For pleasure here and there.
If any man so daring
As dig them up in spite,
He shall find their sharpest thorns
In his bed at night.

Up the airy mountain,
Down the rushy glen,
We daren't go a-hunting
For fear of little men;

Wee folk, good folk,
Trooping all together;
Green jacket, red cap,
And white owl's feather!

William Allingham 1824-1889

The Faerie Portal

Where babbling brook and fishes play
I chanced to walk this summer's day
Alone with every dream and thought
My idle fancy quickly bought.

And there, set in a crumbling wall
A Faerie portal – two feet tall!
Oh Magic Gateway, art thou true?
Or do I just imagine you?

You were not here the other day
When last I walked this ancient way.
What lies beyond your taunting gape?
Faerieland? A dream escape?
A whispering timeless avenue?
And do I dare step through?

Bernie (discovered in the Holybrook).

Faerie Love Song

Human maid: 'Faerie creature, let me know your ways
And hear your magic whispers in my mind.
Let me hear the Starsong all my days
Then I'll leave my human ways behind.'
Faerie male: 'Let me call the lightning down to earth,
Let rolling thunder fill the darkened skies
Let the Sorce surge through my very soul
When I see the love-light in your eyes.'

Bernie

There Are Fairies

There are fairies at the bottom of our garden!
It's not so very, very far away;
You pass the gardener's shed
And you just keep straight ahead
I do so hope they've come to stay.
There's a little wood with moss in it and beetles,
And a little stream that quietly runs through;
You wouldn't think they'd dare
To come merrymaking there,
Well, they do!
There are fairies at the bottom of our garden!
They often have a dance on summer nights;
The butterflies and bees
Make a lovely little breeze,
And the rabbits stand about and hold the lights.
Did you know that they could sit upon the moonbeams
And pick a little star to make a fan,
And dance away up there
In the middle of the air?
Well, they can!

There are fairies at the bottom of our garden!
You cannot think how beautiful they are;
They all stand up and sing
When the fairy queen and king
Come gently floating down upon their car.
The king is very proud and handsome;
The queen, now can you guess who that would be?
She's a little girl all day
But at night she steals away.
Well, it's me!
Rose Fyleman, 1877-1957.
I love this one - written by a girl after my own heart.

The Nocturnal Fae

The dark nocturnal Faerie is handsome to behold
Yet sightings are unlikely because he's far from bold.
He's smaller than a human, yet muscularly compact
His strength is unbelievable, if he should choose to act.

His skin is smooth and creamy pale, his eyes are black as night
And sometimes these can flare with flame to burn you out of sight.
His raven hair is shot throughout with red or green or blue
And sometimes even violet of an iridescent hue.

His wings are black and leathery, just like those of a bat
They span his height and twice again. One beat could knock you flat.
And yet he doesn't often need these pinions to unfold
For he can teleport at will to places yet untold.

His teeth are very white and sharp, his canines elongated
But he won't bite just anyone; he wants you to be mated.
He'll sip your blood with relish, if you are on his level
But if you're not he'll pass you by, he doesn't need a devil.

If you are not 'suitable', you'll be dismissed with scorn
For those who join the Faerie race, they must be purely born.
So can you call him evil – this creature of the night?
He only seeks to live his life, and purify his plight.
Bernie.

Shadows

All around the house is the jet black night
It stares through the window pane.
It crawls in the corners, hiding from the light
And it moves with the moving flame.

And now my little heart goes beating like a drum
With the breath of the bogey in my hair
And all around the candle the crooked shadows come
And go marching along up the stair...

The shadow of the baluster, the shadow of the lamp,
The shadow of the child who goes to bed.
All the wicked shadows coming – tramp, tramp TRAMP
With the black night overhead...
Learned in school C. 1954 – really fired the imagination.

Silvia

Who is Silvia? What is she
That all our swains commend her?
Holy, fair, and wise is she;
The heaven such grace did lend her,
That she might admired be.

Is she kind as she is fair?
For beauty lives with kindness;
Love doth to her eyes repair
To help him of his blindness
And being helped, inhabits there.

Then to Silvia let us sing
That Silvia is excelling;
She excels each mortal thing
Upon the dull earth dwelling:
To her let us garlands bring.
William Shakespeare (just had to include him.)

The Stairs
The door was oak and inches thick; at centre was a lion
Grotesque and black, it mouthed a ring entirely made of iron.
Beyond this door a hallway stretched, gloomy and forboding.
It made me falter, as a child, with senses overloading.

No daylight ever entered here, no windows had been made
Only the light-switch by the door could make me unafraid
To walk the length of this dire stretch and thus to gain the stair
But even there I was not safe on boards so stark and bare.

The stairway creaked on every tread with a moaning kind of sound
I often raced up all six flights, not daring to look round
To see which ghosts I'd wakened with this haunting symphony
Their chilling breath and grinning skulls, clawed hands that reached for
me.
I knew that if I dared to stop, or even worse, to fall
Then ghostly hands might catch me – if they were there at all.
You see, I never turned to look in all my childhood years
So afraid of what I'd see, I failed to face my fears.

Even though I'm old and grey, I still have odd nightmares
In which I never reach the top of endless creaking stairs.
I always wake up with relief, so very glad to know
It wasn't real, and now I'm safe in my tiny bungalow.
Bernie

Twin Spirits

A spirit haunts these Hallowed Halls
The air damply clings to stone built walls
Mouldering curtains threadbare hang.
In the corner dust-laden armour stands.

In the distance floorboards creak
His skin crawls and knees grow weak.
With panting breath and fearful waiting
His whole being is forsaken.

A presence cold, envelopes tight
A long thin hand, transparent, white
Clutches close around his throat
Cutting deep, like a hangman's rope.

None shall come and take Her home
And now this other being will roam.
He now joins her on her ghostly walks.
He too now, other mortals stalk.

Colleen (visiting a house near Dunster)

Overheard on a Salt Marsh

"Nymph, Nymph, what are your beads?"
"Green glass, Goblin. Why do you stare at them?"
"Give them me."
"No."
"Give them me, give them me."
"No."
"Then I will howl all night in the reeds,
Lie in the mud and howl for them."
"Goblin, why do you love them so?"
"They are better than stars or water,
Better than voices of winds that sing,
Better than any man's fair daughter,
Your green glass beads on a silver ring."
"Hush, I stole them out of the moon."
"Give me your beads, I desire them."
"No."
"I will howl in a deep lagoon
For your green glass beads, I love them so,
Give them me. Give them."
"No!"

Harold Monro

Unicorns

A long time ago, when the Earth was green
There was more kinds of animals than you've ever seen
They'd run around free while the Earth was being born
And the loveliest of all was the unicorn.

There was green alligators and long-necked geese
Some humpty backed camels and some chimpanzees
Some cats and rats and elephants, but sure as you're born
The loveliest of all was the unicorn.

The Lord seen some sinning and it gave Him pain
And He says, "Stand back, I'm going to make it rain"
He says, "Hey Noah, I'll tell you what to do
Build me a floating zoo,
And take some of those

Green alligators and long-necked geese
Some humpty backed camels and some chimpanzees
Some cats and rats and elephants, but sure as you're born
Don't you forget My unicorns

Old Noah was there to answer the call
He finished up making the ark just as the rain started to fall
He marched the animals two by two
And he called out as they came through
"Hey Lord,

I've got green alligators and long-necked geese
Some humpty backed camels and some chimpanzees
Some cats and rats and elephants, but Lord, I'm so forlorn
I just can't find no unicorns"

And Noah looked out through the driving rain
Them unicorns were hiding, playing silly games:
Kicking and splashing while the rain was falling
Oh, them silly unicorns.

There was green alligators and long-necked geese
Some humpty backed camels and some chimpanzees
Noah cried, "Close the door because the rain is falling
And we just can't wait for no unicorns"

The ark started moving, it drifted with the tide
The unicorns looked up from the rocks and they cried
And the waters came down and sort of floated them away...
That's why you never see unicorns to this very day.

You'll see green alligators and long-necked geese
Some humpty backed camels and some chimpanzees
Some cats and rats and elephants, but sure as you're born
You're never gonna see no unicorns.
The Bachelors
(Please ignore the bad English – it's a great song and worth preserving).

The Way through the Woods

They shut the road through the woods
Seventy years ago.
Weather and rain have undone it again
And now you would never know
There was once a path through the woods

Before they planted the trees.
It is underneath the coppice and heath
And the thin anemones.
Only the keeper sees
That, where the ring dove broods
And the badgers roll at ease,
There was once a road through the woods.

Yet, if you enter the woods
Of a summer evening late
When the night air cools on the trout-ring'd pools
Where the otter whistles his mate
(They fear not men in the woods
Because they see so few),
You will hear the beat of a horse's feet
And the swish of a skirt in the dew,
Steadily cantering through
The misty solitudes,
As though they perfectly knew
The old lost road through the woods...
But there is no road through the woods.

Rudyard Kipling – 1865-1936

The Witch

The Witch she crept across the room
To grab her dusty witches' broom
So that she could take a flight
Out into the starry night.

No one saw her passing by
Or flying in the darkened sky
Until they heard a witches' cackle
And a frightening, lightning crackle.

And then she flew on straight ahead
And when she got home, she went to bed

Elena Martin

The Wizard

With pointed hat and nails like claws
And a terrible smile on his face
The wizard sits behind locked doors
In his cell in a mountain place.
Around the walls of his magic den
Laid out in endless line
Are books of spells for him to cast
And bottles of magic wine.

With horny hands he waves his wand
And scatters upon the fire
A powder which burns with ghostly light
As the flames rise even higher.
His lips recite a magic spell,
The flames dance on the walls
And shadows deepen on his face
As on his knees he falls.

As I turn the pages of the picture book
The scenes change endlessly
Kings and queens and palaces
And galleons on the sea
But whenever I look at the picture book
I linger at the place
Where the wizard sits behind locked doors
In his cell in a mountain place
With books of spells for him to cast
And bottles of magic wine
And all the time his wicked eyes
Are gazing into mine...

Learned in school c.1954

PRAYERS

Please God...

A Woman's (real) Prayer:

Now I lay me
Down to sleep
I pray the Lord
My shape to keep.
Please no wrinkles
Please no bags
And please lift my butt
Before it sags.
Please no age spots
Please no grey
And as for my belly
Please take it away.
Please keep me healthy
Please keep me young
And thank you Dear Lord
For all that you've done.

Internet

Last Prayer

For all the songs I've never sung
The stories in my head
For all the lines I never wrote
The words I left unsaid.
For all those childhood wishes
That never did come true
For all the dreams I ever dreamed
Of things I never knew.
For all the lies I ever told
And every big mistake
For all the hands I'll never hold
And all the vows I'll break.
For all the hearts I've broken
The loves I've left behind
The healing words unspoken
The darkness in my mind.
For all the times I've never smiled
And all the times I've cried
For all the hardness in my heart
And all the love that died.
For all the days I've wasted
The nights I've tossed and turned
For all the lives I sadly touched
Because I never learned...
Dear Lord, forgive me.

Bernie

Child

The child whispered, "God,speak to me!"
And a meadowlark sang
The child did not hear.

So the child yelled, "God speak to me!"
And the thunder rolled across the sky
But the child did not listen.

The child looked around and said,
"God let me see you" and a star shone brightly
But the child did not notice.

And the child shouted,
"God show me a miracle!"
And a life was born but the child did not know.

So the child cried out in despair,
"Touch me God, and let me know you are here!"
Whereupon God reached down and touched the child.
But the child brushed the butterfly away, and walked away unknowingly.

Anonymous

Dear Lord

I know you're watching over me
And I'm feeling truly blessed
For no matter what I pray for
You always know what's best!

I have this circle of E-mail friends,
Who mean the world to me;
Some days I "send" and "send"
At other times, I let them be.

I am so blessed to have these friends,
With whom I've grown so close;
So this little poem I dedicate to them,
Because to me they are the "Most"!

When I see each name download,
And view the message they've sent;
I know they've thought of me that day,
And "well wishes" were their intent.

So to you, my friends, I would like to say,
Thank you for being a part
Of all my daily contacts,
This comes right from my heart.

God bless you is my prayer today,
I'm honoured to call you "friend"
I pray the Lord will keep you safe,
Until we write again.

Deb xx

Heaven's Special Child

A meeting was held, quite far from Earth—
It's the time again for another birth.
Said the Angels to the Lord above:
"This special child will need much love.
So let's be careful where he's sent
We want his life to be content.
Please, Lord, find the parents who
Will do a special job for you.

His progress will be very slow,
Accomplishments he may not show.
And he'll require much extra care
From the folks he meets down there.
They may not realise it straight away
The special role they are asked to play.
But with this child, sent from above,
Comes stronger faith, and richer love.

He may not talk, or laugh, or play,
His thoughts may seem quite far away.
In many ways he won't adapt—
And he'll be known as 'handicapped'
And soon they'll know the privilege given.
In caring for this gift from Heaven.
Their precious charge, so meek and mild,
Is Heaven's 'Very Special Child'."

Anon

The Holy Alphabet

Although things are not perfect
Because of trial or pain
Continue in thanksgiving
Do not begin to blame
Even when the times are hard
Fierce winds are bound to blow
God is forever able
Hold on to what you know
Imagine life without His love
Joy would cease to be
Keep thanking Him for all the things
Love imparts to thee
Move out of "Camp Complaining"
No weapon that is known
On earth can yield the power
Praise can do alone
Quit looking at the future
Redeem the time at hand
Start every day with worship
To "thank" is a command
Until we see Him coming
Victorious in the sky
We'll run the race with gratitude
Xalting God most high
Yes, there'll be good times and yes some will be bad, but...
Zion waits in glory – where none are ever sad!

Anonymous

I Try

I try but no matter how hard
Whenever I think things are improving
By thought or deed or word
Lady luck turns against me, never moving.

I try starting all over again
From a different angle, maybe winning
But it's all just the same
A new set of heartaches, just beginning.

I try never giving into problems
Hoping my prayers will be answered.
Lord stop where my bad luck stems
Guard me from despair with Your Word.

Colleen

My God

My God, I love thee not because
I hope for heaven thereby,
Nor yet because who love thee not
Are lost eternally.
Not with the hope of gaining aught,
Not seeking a reward
But as thyself hast loved me,
Oh ever-loving Lord.

Saint Francis Xavier

Please Bless my Computer

Dear Lord
Every evening
As I'm lying here in bed
This tiny little prayer
Keeps running through my head

God bless my family
And bless my little pup
And look out for the ones I love
When things aren't looking up

And God, there's one more thing
I wish that you could do
Hope you don't mind me asking
But please bless my computer too?

Now I know that's not normal
To bless a mother board
But just listen a second
While I explain to you 'My Lord'

You see, that little metal box
Holds more to me than odds & ends
Inside those small compartments
Rest a hundred of my 'BEST FRIENDS'

I know for sure they like me
By the kindness that they give
And this little scrap of metal
Is how I travel to where they live

By faith is how I know them
Much the same as you
I share in what life brings them
From that our friendship grew

PLEASE Take an extra minute
From your duties up above
To bless this scrap of metal
That's filled with so much love!

Internet

Twelve Apostles

Peter and Andrew were brothers
James and young John were two others.
James the Less was a writer
Simon the Zealot, a fighter.
Bartholemew was an ordin'ry Jew
And Philip, we guess was one too.
Matthew, we know was a taxman
And Thomas said, "Give me the facts, man."
Thaddeus' role is unclear
He's confused with Judas, we hear
But these days we've learned he was Jude
And some kind of helpless old dude.
So we pray to him now and again,
When hopeless we feel, yes Amen!
But Judas renowned as a traitor
Was replaced by Matthias much later.

Bernie (written for Mum to help her remember)

TIME

Earth time, calendar and seasons too

January

The snowdrop is the promise of new life
That tiny spark of purity against all mundane strife.
We humans make our resolutions, knowing all good faith.
We'll do it right this year, we promise, to ourselves we saith
We'll give up smoking, go on diets
Love our neighbours too.
It's not that we're bad people,
We really want to do –
The right thing, yes the right thing
Our lives to so improve
So why does this not ever work
Are we too dumb to move?
Consider us the snowdrop
Growing bravely through the snow.
Perhaps there is a lesson here
That each of us should know.

Bernie's version

January

Oh lovely month of cold crisp snow
Of wonderful bare trees where sunsets glow.
Frozen streams and brittle white grass
Deep-ploughed ruts, where dark soil lasts.
Ducks and swans slide on thick solid ice.
Short daylight, flashing by in a trice.
Childish voices calling, echoing, shrill
Silent river, as the wheel holds fast at the mill.
Rich blue skies shining through branches
Reflecting on icicles, as the sunlight dances.
A promise of spring will come soon
Till then crackling twigs, under the moon.
January the first month of the year
This wonderful new fresh beginning is here.

Colleen's version

A Burns Night Celebration Oh Yeah!
Ode tae a Fart

Oh what a sleekit horrible beastie
Lurks in your belly efter the feastie
Just as ye sit doon among yer kin
There sterts to stir an enormous wind
The neeps and tatties and mushy peas
Stert workin like a gentle breeze
But soon the puddin wi the sauncie face
Will have ye blawin all ower the place

Nae matter whit the hell ye dae
A'body's gonnae hiv tae pay
Even if ye try tae stifle
It's like a bullet oot a rifle
Hawd yer bum tight tae the chair
Tae try and stop the leakin air
Shifty yersel fae cheek tae cheek
Prae tae God it doesnae reek

But aw yer efforts go assunder
Oot it comes like a clap o thunder
Ricochets aroon the room
Michty me a sonic boom
God almighty it fairly reeks
Hope I huvnae shit my breeks
Tae the bog I better scurry
Aw whit the hell it's no ma worry

A'body roon aboot me chokin
Wan or two are nearly bokin
I'll feel better for a while
Cannae help but raise a smile
Wiz him! I shout with accusin glower
Alas too late, he's just keeled ower
Ye dirty bugger they shout and stare
A dinnae feel welcome any mair

Where e'ere ye go let yer wind gan' free
Sounds like just the job fur me
Whit a fuss at rabbie's party
Ower the sake o one wee farty.

A. Scott (for want of any further information)

February

February rain overfills the ditches
Grass is spongy with mud underneath.
There's one or two snowdrops blooming
Dripping scrubland there on the heath.

The birds flying low over woodland
Dark clouds rolling away cross the hills.
Cattle lowing, calling each softly
Now and again hear Curlew trills.

Late mornings, still holding their darkness
And again, when the workers return home.
There's a silver lining around cloud formations
With the promise of warm springtime to come.

Colleen

Mad March

Will come in with a rush and clouds that race
Then daffy-down-dillies all over the place.
They won't mind the wind; they'll bravely sway
Their golden flags for Saint David's day.
Then on the 3rd when the moon is full
There's a total eclipse like a great ball of wool.
The moon will not vanish, much to our surprise
Just go red and fuzzy before our eyes.
The Ides will come next that were Caesar's demise
When pink and white blossom's shown off by the trees.
So walk round all ladders, make way for black mogs
And rescue those spiders from bathtubs and bogs.
Comic Relief will come round once more
With quizzes and jokes and with funnies galore.
So let's brush up our humour and shake off the woes
As we proudly display that delightful red nose.
Saint Paddy of Ireland is next in our sights
He didn't care much for the *Animal Rights*.
He kicked all the snakes out of Ireland we hear.
He didn't like them, but he did like the beer.
Mothering Sunday is next brought to mind
When all to their mothers must be very kind.
It's the 18th this year, the fourth Sunday in Lent.
So you have no excuse to forget this event.
The first day of spring is officially now,
As the equinox comes and the earth takes a bow.
Equally shared are the day and the night
And Aries begins its impetuous flight.
To the end of the month when schools will outbreak
For kids to have Easter eggs and chocolate cake.

Bernie (2006)

April

A gentle month of rain it seems when flowers rule the land
The bluebells in the woods are best, they look so blue and grand
Like a swaying ocean, thus usurping each wood clearing
A haze of blue assails our eyes in every way endearing.

We never thought when we were young and gathered by the armful
Yet now it is forbidden to pick wild-flowers – was it harmful?
I don't think so, for each of us has placed roots in our garden
To thus preserve and wonder at this species so to harden.

It isn't fair, I know that, even though we try to save
The Nanny State would want us over concrete walls to rave.
But if you are like me and think that Nature is the best
Then keep on picking bluebells for your garden and the rest.

Bernie's version

The Bluebells
Martin's version

They come at an appointed time
Known only to the woodland gods
And certain birds, who shout the odds
When England shucks its overcoat
And sheds the scarf from round its throat
As freed from winter discipline
The spring goes pirouetting in
To raise the bluebells from the ground
This army, shiny from the rain
Which rose so quietly overnight
Encamped here by the morning light
In serried ranks of sapphire blue
And growing thicker by the day
As April catches up with May

And where the light-shards lie once more
In leopard-prints on leaf-mould floor
Strewn there by a reckless sun
The muntjac deer start up and run
And squirrels bicker in their drays
As blackthorn blossom snows the ways
A joke on winter sketched by spring
On staves left out from coppicing
While all this time, the eyesight bathes
In iridescent bluebell swathes.

Martin Newell (Sunday Express)

May

It comes in like a lion, they say
And goes out like a lamb.
We've heard of things like 'Darling buds'
And others not so glam.

We've heard you shouldn't 'shed a clout'
Whatever that might mean
Until this fickle month is out
Then have a grand spring-clean.

We think it possibly refers
To blossom of the may
Rather than the month itself
In all its sweet array.

May gives us two Bank Holidays,
A rare treat for our kind.
One May-day and one Whitsun.
You wouldn't think we'd mind.

They say the month is 'merry'
I don't know why they should.
P'raps it's steeped in history
And the Green Man of the wood.

Bernie

June Poppy

Behold the ragged Princess of the Dawn!
In scarlet silk she whispers in the corn
And reminds us to remember...

Bernie

June's Secret Garden

I came into a deep remembered garden
It was like I awoke from pain.
I heard the song of a blackbird singing
And the sound of the brook babbling in the rain.

I felt a soft June breeze upon my skin
The moon gently began to rise.
I turned and thought I saw you standing there
With tender love shining in your eyes.

Colleen

July

The trees are truly green right now
The summer's in full flow.
Most people take their holidays
To far-off venues go.

But really there is not a need
To waste your money so.
This island here has everything
From summer sun to snow.

We've got mountains in the Highlands
And beaches all around.
We've got waterfalls and forests
And moors that so abound.

Or if you're into history
Or how we lived before
There're hundreds of majestic homes
Your whim to such explore.

Yes, Britain does have everything
I really shouldn't gloat.
Just let me have a Scottish glen
With a castle and a moat.

I think I will retire there
Some day in future time.
I think it suits me very well
This land of mine sublime.

Bernie

August
A time of golden harvests
And huge great moons that rise
Just over the horizon
Like super pumpkin pies.

It hasn't rained much lately,
We've got a hose-pipe ban
But somehow our dear gardens
Survive the best they can.

There're loads of plums upon the trees
And apples yet to swell.
The smoke from many barbecues
Soon fills the air as well.

The wasps can be quite irksome
When you eat your food outside
Those little pesky horrors
From which you cannot hide.

A further holiday this month,
So who are we to moan?
It's time for sun and holidays
To which our culture's prone.

Bernie

Late September

Not many takers for this month

Tang of fruitage in the air;
Red boughs bursting everywhere;
Shimmering of seeded grass;
Hooded gentians all a'mass.

Warmth of earth, and cloudless wind
Tearing off the husky rind,
Blowing feathered seeds to fall
By the sun-baked, sheltering wall.

Beech trees in a golden haze;
Hardy sumachs all ablaze,
Glowing through the silver birches.
How that pine tree shouts and lurches!

From the sunny door-jamb high,
Swings the shell of a butterfly.
Scrape of insect violins
Through the stubble shrilly dins.

Every blade's a minaret
Where a small muezzin's set,
Loudly calling us to pray
At the miracle of day.

Then the purple-lidded night
Westering comes, her footsteps light
Guided by the radiant boon
Of a sickle-shaped new moon.

From Sword Blades and Poppy Seeds By Amy Lowell

October

We've had the Harvest Moon by now
And nights are drawing in.
The fruit has vanished off the trees
The windfalls are a sin.

The autumn leaves are falling
From the trees all red and gold.
They crunch beneath our every step
A childhood joy of old.

There're conkers and there're acorns
For every child to please.
Do not deny these ancient joys
For Nanny State appease.

And soon it will be Hallowe'en
For every child's delight.
They get to dress up gruesomely
And give us all a fright.

Okay, I know it rains a lot,
But who are we to moan?
It's Nature's plan to feed the earth
That we suppose we own.

Bernie

Clocks Back

A heartbeat shatters
At the radio dawn.
Identities scatter
At the starter horn.

It's time to eat
Now it's time to yawn
This time of year
Is the best to be born.

You're early; you're late
You are right on time.
One day I'll get round
To fixing this watch of mine.

No wonder you're down
Did you sleep all right?
The clocks turned around
Time went backwards last night.

But who tells the sun
And who tells the moon
We put back the clocks
And you're shining too soon?

If they did it all the time
You'd be old before you were born
And before the start of time
All the clocks would be worn.

David Brewster

November

The fireworks greet us every night
Exploding all around.
Sometimes it seems like overhead
They're bombing us with sound.

Now don't think I'm a killjoy
Or anything like that.
But aren't they s'posed to please the eye
Not knock our houses flat?

We're s'posed to be a nation
Of pet-lovers they say.
So how can we forgive ourselves
By frightening them this way?

Imagine if you were a dog
Or even a fine cat,
With hearing magnified ten times
What would you think of that?

To firework manufacturers
I cannot understand
Why something meant for beauty
Has got so out of hand.

Oh, I know that there are fine displays
Which certainly I love.
So why insist on ruining it
With deafness from above?

I wish that I were in control
I sure would make it law
To ban all deafening fireworks
For now and evermore.

Bernie

November the 5th 2004

The sparks from the fire flew out of sight
The guy on the fire burned on bonfire night.
Fireworks exploded one after another
As we stood in awe, me and my brother.
The crackle of wood glowed in the dark,
Eager faces smiling as we crowded the park.
The north wind blew cold in our backs
You could see in the leaves, our muddy tracks.
The smell of baking potatoes in jackets
The cheering crowd making a racket.
The fire died down after burning so bright
We'd oh, such fun on this bonfire night!

Colleen

TRAVEL

Come along with us...

Bath

Bath, fair city of terraced stone
With curves and circles in symmetrical row.
This upsurge in my breast for you alone
To gaze in wonder and inwardly know.

From my childhood of long hot summers
In winters of fun, in snow and rain.
To my youth full of pain and stirring murmurs
I shall never see and feel that way again.

The valley between those hills of green
The Romans saw when they found the spa
And sowed the seeds of glory seen
Bought their art, to adorn from afar.

Through the ages came Nash, Allen and Wood
Each leaving their mark, richly bestowed.
Everything blending, elegantly good
From the warmth of the stone to where Avon flowed.

Now the abbey casts its shadow around
To all the passages, alleys and nooks
Across where a thriving commerce is found
Shops full of art, antiques, treasures and books.

Great Pultney Street leads to its stylish end
To Sydney Gardens, full of shrubs and bridges
Where everyone, meets everyone's friends
Down between the railway's tunnels and ridges.

To be beckoned by one so elegant
I fill with pride as I look around.
Oh! wondrous Bath to you I'm bound.

Colleen

A Bike with No Name

A recent survey found that 81% of parents banned their children from unsupervised cycling because of safety fears

It was second-hand and basic.
A battered old blue frame;
Whoever used to own it
Had painted out the name.

A cricking leather saddle,
Two pedal rubbers gone,
My grandad fixed the cables
And put the brake blocks on,

Some rim tape, a reflector
And various other parts
And off I went to London
From Harpenden in Herts.

A puncture kit, a sandwich,
About thirteen years old,
The A5 and North Circular'
The route that I'd been told.

And yes, in heavy traffic
And no, not quite as bad,
But no one said my parents
Were negligent or mad.

I never wore a helmet;
It didn't end in tears,
A kid in central London,
A bike that had no gears.

Would never happen these days;
Their parents say they can't,
That accidents are rising,
Though figures say they aren't.

So here's a new solution
For traffic in the town;
Fill the roads with school kids.
That should calm it down.

Martin Newell

Elvis – Never Been to London

Did those feet in blue suede shoes
Ever pace our pavements grey?
Had the holy lamé god
Come to England for a day,
Sampled '50s fish 'n chips
All washed down with PG Tips?

What might he have made of us?
Pinstripe suits and bowler hats,
Staring from a London bus
Over blocks of council flats
Like the ghost of rock 'n' roll
In a fog of fags and coal.

Did he pass himself off then
As some ordinary chap?
Gazing out across Big Ben,
Instant coffee and evap,
While the waitress serving tea
Told herself it couldn't be.

Was he even here at all?
Curling lip and hair jet black
In that phone box by the wall
Waiting for his pennies back,
After pressing Button B
Elvis calling Tennessee.

No, the King did not appear;
Never saw the guy round here.
Still the legend lingers on
And the mystery train has gone.

Martin Newell

Bussing it

The sun comes up like a bloody great orange
Silvery jet-trails zip up the sky
As if such pale fragility might fall apart, or try.
Every inanimate object is sugared with frost
Except where feet have trodden
Hands have brushed, or wheels criss-crossed.
At every stop, a huddle of cold humanity
Fidgeting, stamping,
Breathing hot vapours of impatience
Like fettered horses, eager to be gone.
Each one boards with tangible relief
Red noses, watered eyes
Fumbling for change with cold fingers
While those behind refrain from rushing on.
The mood is lighter now in such brief solace
A little warmth, a seat, some friendly chat.
"Hello, how are you? Ain't it cold?"
"This blooming bus is always bloody late!"
The sun is higher now, more like a coppered disc.
The frost's receding wetly in the shine.
The bus fills up as journey's end approaches
From end to end, those standing form a line.
The mood is not so jovial now, we find

As bodies like sardines begin to grind
Upon each other's nerves, as the bus jolts and swerves.
Sheer weight of numbers makes it such a bind.
And I have got to get off next – I frown
Long before we reach the favoured town
Through throngs of irate bodies I must fight
Before I can in confidence alight.
But when I finally make it, I am free
The clear, cold morning seems to welcome me
Alone, unfettered – what a treat it seems.
Ten minutes I must walk with just my dreams
And no more buses till the evening stint...

Bernie (when she used to make the incredible journey of 4 miles that took 1½ hours).

Exile

Asleep among the dustbins
I heard a seabird cry,
"Wake up you workless vagabond
It's emigrate or die!
The bugs rule all the bedclothes
TB stalks through the room.
Set sail for 'Pagan England'
Or stay to meet your doom."

Awake among the dustbins
I heard that seagull's cry.
I knew I must leave Dublin
A tear came to my eye.
I sailed the sea of misery
My heart filled with despair,
When behold! In 'Pagan England'
A kinder God found there.

Eammon Buckley

Kathy's Song

I hear the drizzle of the rain
Like a memory it falls
Soft and warm continuing
Tapping on my roof and walls.

And from the shelter of my mind
Through the window of my eyes
I gaze beyond the rain-drenched streets
To England where my heart lies.

My mind's distracted and diffused
My thoughts are many miles away
They lie with you when you're asleep
And kiss you when you start your day.

And as a song I was writing is left undone
I don't know why I spend my time
Writing songs I can't believe
With words that tear and strain to rhyme.

And so you see I have come to doubt
All that I once held as true
I stand alone without beliefs
The only truth I know is you.

And as I watch the drops of rain
Weave their weary paths and die
I know that I am like the rain
There but for the grace of you go I.

Paul Simon

London Marathon

Only last year I started to run
Just a mile or two, a bit of fun.
Longer and tougher the distance became
Through snow and ice, wind and rain.
Dark winter evenings pounding the road
Forcing my legs into running mode.

Sunday mornings, no lying in
Out in the cold to get the miles in.
Now here I stand in the starting pack
Thousands of runners, front and back.
Boom! That's it; we're off at last
Nice and easy not too fast.

One eye on the clock checking the time
Eight minutes a mile and feeling fine.
Children's hands held out to say
'Give me five then be on your way.'
One quick stop to have a pee
By a factory wall in Bermondsey.

Then over the Thames and past halfway
Race leaders passing the other way.
Round the docks and then it hits
My rhythm suddenly falls to bits.
Twenty miles gone; I feel so slow
Still six weary miles to go.

I can't go on; my legs are lead
Shouldn't be here, and could be in bed.
My body demands that I should stop
Or else will face my final drop.
So I obey and start to walk
I don't care if people talk.

All that training down the drain
A cloudy mist envelops my brain.

A marshal sees my plight and roars
'Come on, dig deep – find some more!
You know it's there somewhere inside.'
And through my haze I pick up my stride.

The pain must be etched across my face.
If it kills me I'll finish this bloody race.
And then at last I'm in the Mall.
Oh thank you, God, my mate, my pal.
Across the line with arms held high
Head flopped back to face the sky.

Then people ask, 'How long did you take?'
I say, 'Three hours forty – piece of cake.
Ran all the way and didn't slow.'
But you and me, we know it ain't so.
Not one achievement today, but two.
I'm not sure which was harder to do.
Got my medal; it's in the bag –
And lasted four hours without a fag!

Tony Bennett

Reality

Sitting here, on an underground train
Speeding through the night, speeding through the rain.
I read a newspaper I found on my seat
Left here by a stranger that I will never meet.

I scan the pages, I read the headlines
Same old stories, same old crimes.
All of them written to their deadlines
Busy people, busy lives.

I look out my window; there's not much to see
A few city lights and a reflection of me.
It's 5.am and I'm on my way home
But when I get there I'll still be all alone.

No-one to hold me and say 'I love you'
Just me and my TV
No-one for me to come home to
There's nobody but me.

Jane Quittenton

Sea-Fever

I must down to the seas again, to the lonely sea and the sky,
And all I ask is a tall ship and a star to steer her by,
And the wheel's kick and the wind's song and the white sail's shaking,
And a grey mist on the sea's face, and a grey dawn breaking.
I must down to the seas again, for the call of the running tide
Is a wild call and a clear call that may not be denied;
And all I ask is a windy day with the white clouds flying,
And the flung spray and the blown spume, and the sea-gulls crying.
I must down to the seas again, to the vagrant gypsy life,
To the gull's way and the whale's way where the wind's like a whetted
knife;
And all I ask is a merry yarn from a laughing fellow-rover
And quiet sleep and a sweet dream when the long trick's over.

John Masefield (English Poet Laureate, 1930-1967)

Steam on the Track

Crossing the bridge by Kemps Eye Farm,
I look down on the track –
Oh how I wish that someone great
Could bring the steam trains back.

I hear again the whistles shrill;
I see the gleaming brass
And hear the hissing jets of steam
As 'Kings' and 'Castles' pass.

Great clouds of smoke envelop me
As on the bridge I stand.
They glide and drift like awesome crests
Across the nearby land.

I glimpse the open firebox and
The orange glow inside,
And the driver with his fireman
Working with skill and pride.

The air is acrid to the taste;
Black smuts fly everywhere,
But honestly there's nothing now
That with steam can compare.

They were seldom late or faulty
And, if one chanced to be,
There was always a known reason
For a freak deformity!

Sometimes I stand on Kemps Eye Bridge,
Heedless of cold or rain,
Waiting to see and hear and smell
A steam engine again.

And as it passes, history
Is borne along the track.
My very being fills with pride
As memories flood back.

Mary Lacey

Not our favourite section. But the experience must be included

Air raid

The night was calm and still.
Suddenly, from around the hill
Heavy shadows droning near
Filling all my world with fear.
Sirens building higher, shrill.
Has Gerry not yet had his fill?
Coming from shelter to streets of dust
Everything now, with choking crust.
Stumbling over rubble wide
A screaming hoarseness, deep inside.
Clawing at the smouldering heap
Terrified of what I'd find beneath.

Colleen on Bath air raids

The Old Pole
(In 1962)
They've taken her away from wandering the streets outcast.
She didn't mean to grab the knife
But she thought she was fighting for her children's life.
Again she saw the camp wires closing around her
The smell of burning flesh surrounds her.
Uniforms and black boots stamp around
She fell screaming to the ground.
Gently, men in white coats
And strong hands, tenderly lift
Another victim, of the Nazi gift.

*Colleen on a neighbour when workmen tried to change her flat over
from coal gas*

Patrick

Watching my brother, my eyes smarted with tears
As he marched in the parade, remembering over the years
His mates from his childhood, life stopped before hardly begun.
So he 'signed on' under age to do what they wanted done.
He'd been on minesweepers on seas of chaos and fear
He survived death, bloodshed, destruction and was still here.
He was remembering 'the lads' with their once laughing eyes
Their jokes, silly games and their friendship ties.
He'd since lived for them, a life full of joy
He was thinking now of his friends as a boy.

Colleen

Universal Soldier

He's five foot-two, and he's six feet-four;
He fights with missiles and with spears.
He's all of thirty-one, and he's only seventeen,
Been a soldier for a thousand years.

He's a Catholic, a Hindu, an Atheist, a Jain,
A Buddhist and a Baptist and a Jew.
And he knows he shouldn't kill
And he knows he always will,
Kill you for me my friend and me for you.

And he's fighting for Canada,
He's fighting for France,
He's fighting for the USA,
And he's fighting for the Russians,
And he's fighting for Japan,
And he thinks we'll put an end to war this way.

And he's fighting for Democracy,
He's fighting for the Reds,
He says it's for the peace of all.
He's the one who must decide,
Who's to live and who's to die,
And he never sees the writing on the wall.

But without him
How would Hitler have condemned him at Dachau?
Without him Caesar would have stood alone.
He's the one who gives his body
As a weapon of the war
And without him all this killing can't go on.

He's the Universal Soldier and he really is to blame;
His orders come from far away no more.
They come from here and there and you and me
And brothers can't you see
This is not the way we put the end to war.

Donovan

WORK

Said to be good for the soul

Advertising
The spider lays a thousand eggs
The hen, she lays just one.
The spider never cackles
To tell us what she's done.
And yet we prize the bonny hen
And spider we despise
Which only goes to show you
It pays to advertise!
Bernie

Factory Girl
Monday morning
Back to her machine
Time takes its time
More time for a daydream.
In the fumes and noise
Her senses are numb
She only hears the bell
Waits for a friend to come.
It's a different story
By the coffee machine
An oasis of laughter
"Where have you been?"
In the back of her mind
Her foreman's eyes
Count the seconds
As the talk goes by.
A conversation
Can last for a day
All the faces she knows
Take the boredom away.
Another Monday over
She hears the last bell.
In four more years
She'll be free of this hell.
But she'll still be working

Just the same
Walking the kids to school
In the pouring rain.
There are no bells now
There is not much time
Her mind ticks like thunder
To make sure it's all fine.
Then her daughter leaves school
To be a factory girl
Daydreaming her mornings
She awaits a new world.

Dave Brewster

The Gardener

Looking at the view with gardener's eye
He saw work and care of days gone by.
The green of plants, trees and lawns
Planted long before he was born.

His heart aching and pounding with joy
Remembering days when he was a boy
Of all the pleasure and toil
Now at peace and one with the soil.

His hands, now gnarled and old
Still held strongly and bold
The master tools of his trade
Working in the sun or shade
He is part of all he surveys
And will be so till the end of his days.

Colleen (written at Englefield House)

Just 17

I wake up early in the morning
Switch off my alarm.
I can't stop yawning.
Mum comes in with a cup of tea
Puts on the light
I can hardly see.
Pull back the bedclothes
God – it's cold
Makes me feel I'm getting old.
I'm in the bathroom
I wash and dress
I think of my life
It's such a mess
Just 17 – it's such a waste
She thinks as she makes for the door in haste.
As I'm walking down the street
There's not a soul
No-one to meet.
My footsteps echo all around
No other noise
Not a sound.
I get on the bus
Find my seat
Put down my bag and rest
My feet.

Jane Quittenton (17)

Ol' Jed's Song

Come and listen to a story 'bout a man named Jed,
A poor college kid, barely kept his family fed,
But then one day he was talking to a recruiter,
Who said, "they pay big bucks if ya work on a computer..."

Windows, that is... PC's... Workstations...

Well, the first thing ya know ol' Jed's an Engineer.
The kinfolk said "Jed, move away from here".
They said "California is the place ya oughta be",
So he bought some donuts and he moved to Silicon Valley...

Intel, that is... Pentium ... Big amusement park...

On his first day at work, they stuck him in a cube.
Fed him more donuts and sat him at a tube.
They said "your project's late, but we know just what to do.
Instead of 40 hours, we'll work you 52!"

OT, that is... Unpaid... Mandatory...

The weeks rolled by and things were looking bad.
Schedules started slipping and some managers were mad.
They called another meeting and decided on a fix.
The answer was simple... "We'll work him sixty-six!"

Tired, that is... Stressed out... No social life...

Months turned to years and his hair was turning grey.
Jed worked very hard while his life slipped away.
Waiting to retire when he turned 64,
Instead he got a call and escorted out the door.

Laid off, that is... De-briefed... Unemployed...

Now the moral of the story is to listen what you're told,
Companies will use you and discard you when you're old.
So gather up your friends and start your own firm,
Beat the competition, watch the bosses squirm.

Millionaires, that is... Bill Gates... Steve Jobs...

Y'all come back now... Ya hear'

Nice one, Colleen!

Shift Worker
Lights – silver and gold on the blue-grey dawn
Lights of the town still sleeping,
Snug in their beds, still warm.
Only the birds bravely greeting
Their songs fill the silence.
Only the birds and I greet the brand-new morn.
Bernie

Spell-checker

I have a spelling checker.
It came with my PC.
It plane lee marks four my revue
Miss steaks aye can knot see.
Eye ran this poem threw it.
Your sure real glad two no.
Its very polished in its weigh,
My checker tolled me sew.
A checker is a blessing.
It freeze yew lodes of thyme.
It helps me right awl stiles two reed,
And aides me when aye rime.
Each frays comes posed up on my screen
Eye trussed too bee a joule.
The checker pours o'er every word
To cheque sum spelling rule.
Bee fore a veiling checkers
Hour spelling mite decline,
And if we're laks oar have a laps,
We wood bee maid too wine.
Butt now bee cause my spelling
Is checked with such grate flare,
There are know faults with in my cite,
Of nun eye am a wear.
Now spelling does not phase me,
It does knot bring a tier.
My pay purrs awl due glad den
With wrapped words fare as hear.
Of witch won should be proud,
And wee mussed dew the best wee can,
Sew flaws are knot aloud.
Sow ewe can sea why aye dew prays
Such soft wear four pea seas,
And why eye brake in two averse
Buy righting want too please.

Internet

Slave

Up at seven or very close; quick cup of tea and piece of toast
Off I rush like so many others: builders, teachers, doctors, mothers.
Only one thing on my mind – get to work and face the grind
No matter what's in store today, I'll get it done to earn my pay.
Criticisms from my boss; really he doesn't give a toss
He's just doing the same as me: slaving to feed his family
Paying off his monthly dues, buying his daughter ballet shoes.
I don't want designer clothes, or sporty car in which to pose
Yet I am forced to live this way, compromising every day.
Not much leisure time for me; pleasure and fun are secondary.
So on it goes; no end in sight. I ask myself is all this right?
Why must I exist like this?
I guess that's just the way it is.

Tony Bennett

Waking Up with a Clock Radio

Oh, I hate getting up in the morning
How I hate getting out of my bed
But in spite of my grunting and yawning
That beeping gets inside my head.
I open one eye at the 'larm clock
And glower it with murd'rous intent
But it don't take a blind bit of notice
Just carries on like it just went.

Till fin'lly I'm goaded to action
And reach for the button to choose –
The one in the middle, I think it should be
The one that invites you to snooze...
But sadly, I miss it completely
Erratic'ly short of my goal
Instead I depress the one on the left
And get blasted with loud Rock 'n Roll!

Once the bane of my life – Bernie

Worker

I'm Nobody, but Everyone on every factory floor
A robot or a chimpanzee could do my job or more.
I'm just a component – a cog in the wheel
I don't have emotions and can't even feel.
But without me my nation would fall flat on its face
I'm a Hero, a Superman, the Saviour of my race.
So don't you try to tell me you're a better man than I
You with your white collar and your Company tie.
It's ME who pays your wages, and keeps those on the dole
It's me who keeps the Royalty in diamonds, furs and Rolls.
Don't bother to converse with me 'bout politics and such
I just don't have the time, mate
I'm earnin' much too much.

Bernie

25 Years
(written to Colleen)
A quarter century is long – long enough for most
Yet you have stuck it out quite well – here at the Evening Post.
We often wondered how you managed. Is it gluttony?
Or is it just a natural gift to cope eternally?

So many faces you have seen, to come and soon to go
It must seem a kaleidoscope of people you don't know.
So many people you have helped over all the years
So many melodramas – so many laughs and tears.

If you could have your time again, we wonder if you'd mind
Or if you'd take your shining gifts – and leave us all behind.
Who else would have a sewing kit – and know the words of law?
Who else would put our spellings right and kick our butts galore?
Bernie

Finale

We're gathered together to wish you good cheer
For some it's 'Goodbye' though you'll still be quite near.
You've worked in this office for many a year
With quite a few giggles, some frowns or a tear.

Though the changes you've seen have been massive and wide
You tackled them bravely – took all in your stride.
Many faces have come and gone over the years,
For loads have moved on to pursue grand careers.

And these won't forget you – they're daft if they should
They owe quite a lot to one faithful and good.

If ever the workload was too much to bear
You managed quite well not to cuss or to swear.

Yes, always your humour has carried you through
The workplace was richer for 'heroes' like you.
Bronwyn was your mascot – that cute little sheep
We'll make sure she lives on – her memory will keep.

It's all down to respect and the stuff that you 'feel'
Like Ali G says, "You've got to get real."
You taught a great lesson to all Admin folk
We were just born to help – and it sure is no joke.

From the young and the old, and those in between
Everybody will miss you, our 'Scrutineer Queen'.

(written to Colleen on her retirement)

The Two Bronnies

We're off to pastures new
Bronwyn has finally found her way home
So it's 'Goodbaa' from ME
And 'Goodbaa' from 'ER.

Luv from Bernie and Colleen xx